Yosemite

Kate Nearpass Ogden

REAKTION BOOKS

This book is dedicated to Warren, my husband and editor of many years, and to Emma, Claire and Lucy, our daughters. When they were younger, the twins' dance on Glacier Point Cliff was so distracting that the Yosemite park ranger giving a tour had to ask them to stop. The book is also dedicated to my parents, Bonita and Charlie, who would have been pleased with the mix of art, history and science contained within its pages.

Published by Reaktion Books Ltd
33 Great Sutton Street
London EC1V 0DX, UK
www.reaktionbooks.co.uk

First published 2015
Copyright © Kate Nearpass Ogden 2015

Printed and bound in China

A catalogue record for this book is available
from the British Library

ISBN 978 1 78023 527 1

Contents

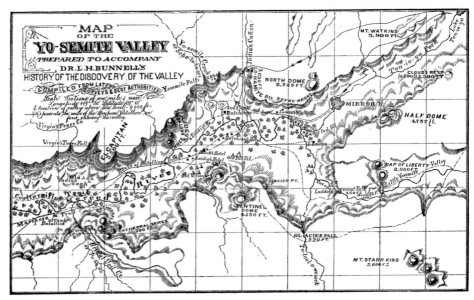

'Map of the Yo-semite Valley', engraving from L. H. Bunnell,
Discovery of the Yosemite (1892 edn).

ONE

Granite Plutons and 'God's Great Plow'

In the Sierra Nevada mountains of California lies Yosemite Valley, a scenic wonder famous for its unusual geological formations, numerous waterfalls and spectacular vistas. Dubbed 'the incomparable valley' by the geologist François E. Matthes, Yosemite (pronounced yo-*seh*-mi-tee) presents more unusual features than nearly any other location of comparable size. As one nineteenth-century writer noted, 'Yo Semite is the crowding of a multitude of romantic, peculiar, and grand scenes within a very small space.'[1]

Yosemite Valley was millennia in the making, yet was discovered the geological equivalent of a split second ago. When the valley was first seen by Anglo-American eyes in the nineteenth century, the discussion of its origins probably began a literal heartbeat later. In this book, I have undertaken a cultural history of this spectacular natural site, beginning with the geological forces that created its unusual formations and ending with the park's present-day status as a national playground visited by millions of tourists and sports enthusiasts every year.

Yosemite Valley extends in an east–west orientation. When visitors arrive at the valley's open western end, they are greeted by the 'Gates of the Valley': a sheer cliff named El Capitan on the left or north side, and a granite wall adorned with a graceful waterfall known as Bridalveil on the right or south side. El Capitan rises a majestic 900 metres (3,000 feet) while Bridalveil Fall leaps 190 metres (620 feet) to the valley floor.

As visitors move eastward up the valley, a succession of distinctive features reveal themselves along the north and south walls. Looming above the valley on the north side are three angular, lookalike cliffs called the Three Brothers, followed by three-tiered Yosemite Falls, whose upper fall, cascades and lower fall descend 740 metres (2,425 feet) overall, making it one of the highest waterfalls in the continental United States. Along the south side are a massive, rounded formation named Cathedral Rocks, sharp pinnacles known as Cathedral Spires and a tall, squared-off column called Sentinel Rock.

Huge granite formations known as Half Dome, North Dome, the Royal Arches and Washington's Column buttress the eastern end of the valley. The aptly named Half Dome, the most unusual of these formations and the highest at more than 1,430 metres (4,700 feet), appears to have been sliced neatly in half by some Brobdingnagian blade. At its eastern end, Yosemite also has three small tributary canyons, with the beautiful Mirror Lake located in Tenaya Canyon to the northeast, Vernal and Nevada Falls in Nevada Canyon to the southeast and Illilouette Fall in its namesake valley to the south.

Some of the names given to the Yosemite formations are eminently logical: Half Dome looks exactly like the remaining half of a granite dome that was cleft in two, and North Dome is located along the north wall of the valley. Others were more poetically christened. According to Josiah D. Whitney, State Geologist of California from 1860 to 1874, Sentinel Rock was named for its 'fancied likeness to a

'The Gates of the Valley', El Capitan on the left, Bridalveil Fall on the right.

The Three Brothers, Yosemite, a granite formation consisting of three parallel cliffs: Eagle Peak (the tallest), Middle Brother and Lower Brother.

gigantic watch-tower'.[2] The Three Brothers are overlapping rocks that tilt at the same dramatic angle, and the formation known as Cathedral Spires resembles the pinnacles of a Gothic cathedral. Those same Spires, however, suggested something entirely different to the Native Americans living at Yosemite. As related by one modern writer, 'the two needle-like rocks which tower to the east of Cathedral Rock are *pusi'na*, the squirrel, and *chuk'ka*, the acorn storage granary, forever reminding us of the need to store acorns where animals can't get them'.[3]

Other names bestowed by early visitors are variously poetic or descriptive. Lafayette Houghton Bunnell, one of the first Anglo-Americans to see Vernal and Nevada Falls, named the former for the 'cool, vernal spray' it produces, while the latter was titled 'because it was the nearest to the Sierra Nevada [Mountains]'. James Mason Hutchings, an early Yosemite settler and innkeeper, named Bridalveil

overleaf: The eastern end of Yosemite Valley with Royal Arches, North Dome, Basket Dome and Half Dome, as seen from Glacier Point, 2005.

Fall in 1855, remarking to his travelling companion at the time, 'Is it not as graceful, and as beautiful, as the veil of a bride?'[4]

Some Yosemite appellations were derived from Native American names, although the translations were hit-or-miss. According to one early visitor, Tu-toch-ah-nu-lah, or Tu-tok-a-nu'-la, meant 'the captain' (*el capitan* in Spanish), whereas Galen Clark, a Yosemite innkeeper and guardian of the valley, believed it was a translation of 'inchworm' or 'measuring worm'. Still another source translated Tu-toch-ah-nu-lah as 'Sandhill Crane', the name of a local Indian chief. According to most sources, Tes-sa-ach or Tis-se'-yak – the native designation for Half Dome – was the name of a legendary Indian maiden; in some versions of the legend she was transformed into the mountain itself. Other sources translate the name simply as 'cleft rock'.

Even the translation of the word 'Yosemite' has changed over time. Initially it was thought to be a variation of the Miwok word for 'grizzly bear', an interpretation that held sway for many years. More recently, some writers have suggested that it may be a corruption of the Miwok phrase *johemite*, meaning 'some of them are killers' (perhaps referring to members of another native group).[5] Scholars differ on the derivation of the term, however, and its translation continues to be a subject of debate.[6]

Spellings of the word 'Yosemite' varied widely in the early days, from Yo Hamite to Yo Sem-i-te; several years passed before the name stabilized in its present form. The Miwok called Yosemite Valley 'Awahni', which means 'place like a gaping mouth'. They called the valley's inhabitants 'Awahnichi', or 'people who live in Awahni'. In retrospect, it seems ironic that Yosemite, with its negative connotations, was chosen as the name of the valley rather than the more neutral moniker Awahni. The latter, modernized as 'Ahwahnee', was given to the valley's most elegant hotel when it opened in 1927.

CURRENT GEOLOGICAL THEORY posits that there was once a supercontinent that modern-day scientists have named Rodinia. This supercontinent began to break up due to the processes involved in plate tectonics – the movement of segments of the Earth's crust that ride on top of a softer layer known as the asthenosphere. Some time after Rodinia began to break up, the land that would become Yosemite was formed as sedimentary deposits off the west coast of the North American plate.

Around 220 million years ago, the North American plate collided with the Pacific plate, and the latter was pushed underneath in a process called subduction.[7] Immense heat and pressure underground turned those sedimentary layers into metamorphic rocks. The heat and pressure of subduction also produced magma – molten rock less dense than the rock around it – which rose up or 'intruded' into the overlying metamorphic rocks. These bodies of rising magma solidified as granite 'plutons' under the metamorphic rock, miles below the surface. Some magma in the Yosemite area made it all the way to the surface to become volcanic rock.

Subduction and granite production occurred in 'fits and starts' from about 220 million to 85 million years ago, with the majority of the Yosemite and Sierra Nevada granites created between 105 and 85 million years ago.[8] Granite is an igneous rock formed by the crystallization of magma. It can have a range of compositions, but always contains quartz, potassium feldspar and plagioclase. Most of the Sierra Nevada granites also contain biotite and amphibole.[9] The metamorphic rocks that once covered most of the Sierra Nevada bedrock were stripped away by uplift of the mountains and subsequent erosion. This erosion also exposed the granitic plutons near the surface.

The most noticeable and characteristic rocks in the Yosemite area, including the valley's famous formations, are granite. Yosemite's granite plutons are differentiated from each other according to their mineral composition, texture and grain size. The oldest, located along the Merced River west of the valley, date back 114 million years. Inside the valley is the El Capitan pluton, created 108 million years ago, which formed El Capitan, the Cathedral Rocks and the Three Brothers. A later pluton of Taft granite pushed upward into the El Capitan pluton and is now exposed at Taft Point, Dewey Point and elsewhere. The Half Dome pluton, the youngest in the valley at 87 million years of age, formed much of Glacier Point, the Royal Arches and Half Dome itself.[10]

Exfoliation domes like those at Yosemite are plutons of igneous rock that formed underground as magma, slowly cooling, crystallizing and adjusting to pressure conditions below the surface. The granite was then raised to the surface during a mountain-building event. As

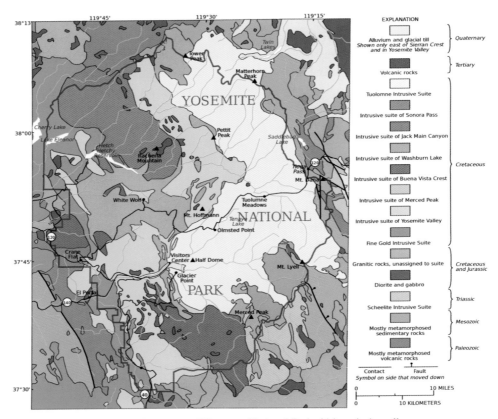

Generalized geologic map of Yosemite National Park. Although the valley
itself is marked 'alluvium and glacial till', it is located within the Yosemite
Valley Intrusive Suite. Glacier Point and Half Dome are located within
the Tuolomne Intrusive Suite.

erosion occurred the pressure was reduced and the granite tended to
expand upward, in the direction of least pressure. During the process of
uplift, residual stresses within the granite formed fractures or sheet joints
parallel to its surface. Water moving along these fractures enhanced
chemical weathering, further weakening the rock. The granite then
eroded in concentric layers, forming rounded masses called exfoliation
domes.

Although exfoliation domes are found worldwide, several excellent
examples are located in the Sierra Nevada Mountains and Half Dome
is the most famous in the United States.[11] The formation called the

Royal Arches, across the valley from Half Dome, offers a cutaway view of granite layers exfoliating in a series of concentric layers. Exfoliation – the erosion of granite in concentric layers, peeling away like the layers of an onion – continues to affect the appearance of Yosemite's domes.

Around 85 million years ago, granite production ceased in the Sierra Nevada region and erosion took over as the leading agent of geological change. Over the course of millions of years, erosion stripped away most of the volcanic material in the area, exposing the granitic rocks and carving deeply into them. During the past ten million years or so, the Sierra Nevada experienced a second major period of uplift, which caused rivers in the area to accelerate their erosion, 'carving the deep bedrock gorges we see at the bottom of many Sierra river canyons'.[12]

Glaciers also played a crucial role in creating the valley. The last glacial period occurred at the end of the Pleistocene era, from approximately 40,000 to 15,000 years ago. Glaciers helped carve valleys in the Sierra Nevada and polished rocks in the area, although they did less to create Yosemite than nineteenth-century geologists believed. The

Edward Weston, *Yosemite, c.* 1938 (Royal Arches, North Dome and Washington's Column), posthumous digital reproduction from original negative.

topography of the region was as much the work of rivers as it was of glacial erosion.

Yosemite's formation was a subject of intense debate in the nineteenth century. With supercontinents and plate tectonics as yet unimagined, the geologists who came to Yosemite promoted their own creation theories, often framing their scientific investigations in religious terms. Writers referred to Yosemite as 'God's laboratory' and called the glacier that had once crept down the valley 'God's great plow'. The valley was also called 'a Scripture of Nature' and 'the voice of God speaking to us through Nature'. Science and religion were considered mutually confirming for much of the nineteenth century, and educated Christians assumed that new scientific discoveries would be reconcilable with religious beliefs already held dear.[13]

The first geologist to propose a theory regarding Yosemite's formation was Josiah D. Whitney. While in his mid-40s, Whitney came to California with a solid record of scientific publications and field experience. Confronted with a valley resembling nothing he had seen in his prior experience, he came up with his own explanation, attributing the initial formation of the granite domes in and around the valley to a process of upheaval. Later in time, at a point when the granite was 'still in a semi-plastic condition below', Whitney theorized that a 'grand cataclysm' caused the bottom of the valley to drop out. The floor subsequently filled in by erosion and sedimentation, resulting in the level meadows located there today.[14] Based partially on known concepts (metamorphic processes, geologic faults and erosion), Whitney's proposal – the 'subsidence' theory – received widespread support in the mid-to-late 1860s.[15]

Whitney was assisted at Yosemite by a younger geologist named Clarence King, who was 21 when he travelled across the country in 1863 with his friend James T. Gardner.[16] The two young men joined Whitney's field team as volunteers. King was many things: a budding scientist who noticed evidence of glacial activity at Yosemite that his employer had overlooked; an explorer who would write exciting accounts of his adventures in the Sierra Nevada; and an educated young man who would become a patron of contemporary painters and photographers. King's field notebooks make it clear that he saw glacial evidence in and around Yosemite Valley and that he considered it more important than Whitney had, but he was reluctant to disagree overtly with his mentor.[17]

Another theory about the formation of the valley was advanced in 1866 by William Phipps Blake, who believed that Yosemite had been produced mainly by slow erosional processes. The valley was, he felt, 'primarily a stream-worn canyon with the final shaping caused by minor glacier action'.[18] Blake, who taught mineralogy and geology at the College of California, had been a rival candidate for the position of State Geologist given to Whitney. By the time he proposed his theory regarding the valley's creation he was teaching at the University of Arizona, and was no longer on site to promote his ideas.

Yet another naturalist who entered the debate was John Muir, an eloquent but relatively unknown young man whose reputation would eventually outshine those of his contemporaries. A throwback to the all-purpose naturalists of an earlier day, he was 30 when he arrived at Yosemite in 1868. Muir found employment as a mill hand and general handyman for the Yosemite innkeeper James Mason Hutchings, maintaining his independence from the state survey and other official agencies.

Muir was more voluble than King in countering Whitney's subsidence theory and positing a gradual change based on accepted, ongoing natural processes such as glaciation and erosion. He published articles, shared his ideas with visitors, and even gave lectures on 'Mountain Sculpture' and 'The Formation of the Yosemite Valley'.[19] Muir not only studied Yosemite, but he made the valley his residence for several years and his spiritual home for the rest of his life.

Over the course of his career, Muir would become known as a preservationist dedicated to protecting natural resources and scenic areas. He endorsed what we would now call a holistic view of the environment. As Muir wrote presciently in 1911, 'When we try to pick out anything by itself, we find it hitched to everything else in the universe.'[20] The glacial interpretation Muir propounded, although refined by geologists since his day, is now confirmed as having come closest to what occurred in the creation of Yosemite Valley.

The next major study of the valley was initiated in 1913 by the United States Geological Survey, with François E. Matthes exploring geomorphology and glacial geology and Frank C. Calkins investigating

Carleton Watkins,
John Muir, c. 1875,
albumen print.

bedrock geology. Matthes determined that Muir's conclusions were more accurate than Whitney's, although he concluded that Muir had overestimated the effects and extent of the glaciers, taking exception to Muir's belief that ice once completely covered the Sierra to the Central Valley and beyond. Matthes also refined the relative roles of rivers and glaciers at Yosemite.[21] One of the most important Yosemite geologists since Matthes was N. King Huber, whose book *The Geologic Story of Yosemite National Park* was published in 1987. A readable geology text for the layman, Huber's book has been reprinted several times.[22]

The most recent investigation of Yosemite's formation, *Geology Underfoot in Yosemite National Park* (2010), was written by Allen Glazner and Greg Stock. Recent developments in geologic theory have added concepts unknown to Yosemite's earlier scientists. The biggest paradigm shifts involve supercontinents and plate tectonics – concepts that have been incorporated into current theories about the valley and its formation.

Geologic change is ongoing at Yosemite. The most dramatic recent events include the large rockfalls of 2008 and 2009. The first occurred near Glacier Point Cliff on 7 and 8 October 2008. A team of scientists studied this event using modern technology, including a combination of gigapixel photography and laser mapping of the cliffs.[23] Their findings indicated that a rock slab 69 metres long (more than 226 feet) and nearly 6,000 cubic metres in volume detached along a sheeting joint parallel to the cliff surface in a clear example of granitic exfoliation. The rockfall damaged structures in Curry Village but caused only minor injuries to its inhabitants. Nearly one-third of the buildings in the village were permanently closed following this rockfall due to the high likelihood of a recurrence.

The rockfall of 2009 occurred at Ahwiyah Point, a smaller peak near Half Dome. According to park geologist Greg Stock, the volume of that rockfall was determined to be 46,700 cubic metres. 'Just over half of that volume consisted of the original block that failed from near the top of Ahwiyah Point,' says Stock, 'while the remainder of the volume was knocked off of the cliff face as the block slid down it. The impact on the cliff generated local seismic shaking equivalent to a magnitude 2.4 earthquake.'[24] The Ahwiyah Point rockfall was the largest at Yosemite since an event in 1987 involving Middle Brother, the middle peak in the Three Brothers formation. During the Middle Brother event, rockfalls occurred twice in one afternoon, bringing down 600,000 cubic metres of rock weighing about 1.3 million metric tons. The rockfall of 1987 remains the largest on record at Yosemite. Rockfalls in 2006 and 2011 temporarily closed the roads leading into the valley.[25]

Although Yosemite was formed over the course of millions of years, it is a 'living organism' still undergoing constant change. In the century and a half since John Muir's arrival, we have come ever closer to understanding the complexity of the valley's geological history.

YOSEMITE'S GRANITE FORMATIONS are best seen from two famous vantage points: Inspiration Point, which offers the first comprehensive view of the valley and is encountered by visitors entering through the Wawona Tunnel, and Glacier Point, located atop Glacier Point Cliff

overleaf: Half Dome, Yosemite, with the wreckage from the Ahwiyah Point rockfall of March 2009 visible at the bottom centre.

on the south side of the valley. The former is the view immortalized in the majority of nineteenth-century paintings and prints, as well as twentieth-century posters and T-shirts. Other scenic vistas, impressive if less comprehensive, can be seen from the trails that ascend the steep walls of the valley.

The many waterfalls located in and around Yosemite compete for tourist attention with the valley's unusual rock formations. Most famous is the iconic Yosemite Falls, a three-tiered configuration of upper fall, cascade and lower fall that has been painted and photographed ever since the valley's first draftsman, Thomas A. Ayres, sketched it in the summer of 1855. Almost as famous is the poetically named Bridalveil Fall, located at the valley's western entrance.

Yosemite's waterfalls reach peak volume in May or June, when spring temperatures melt the snow in the Sierra Nevada Mountains; by August, they are often reduced to a mere trickle. The valley proper is home to an additional three waterfalls: 610-metre (2,000-foot) Sentinel Fall, located just west of Sentinel Rock; 491-metre (1,612-foot) Ribbon Fall, located near Bridalveil; and 305-metre (1,000-foot) Horsetail Fall, located on the east side of El Capitan. The last is best known for its fiery appearance when it reflects the setting sun in mid-to-late February.

Side canyons and more distant locations in the Sierra Nevada contain other waterfalls. Thousands of tourists hike from Yosemite's valley floor into Nevada Canyon to see Nevada and Vernal Falls, which measure 181 and 97 metres (594 and 317 feet), respectively. Other examples, including Illilouette Fall in Illilouette Canyon, are only visible to hikers on mountain trails. Hetch Hetchy Valley – famous among environmentalists for John Muir's unsuccessful campaign to save it from conversion into a reservoir – once contained waterfalls and rock formations remarkably similar to those in Yosemite. Wapama, Tueeulala and Rancheria Falls are still visible today above the water level of the reservoir.

In addition to its granite formations and scenic waterfalls, Yosemite is home to a wide variety of flora and fauna. The park includes five different vegetation zones, with a correspondingly wide variety of plant life. These zones vary according to elevation, from the Foothill-Woodland Zone (located on the western boundary of the park at El Portal) through

View from Inspiration Point, Yosemite, also called 'Tunnel View' (view from the exit of the Wawona Tunnel). El Capitan on the left, Bridalveil Fall on the right.

the Lower Montane Forest (beginning 910 metres/3,000 feet above sea level), the Upper Montane Forest (1,830 metres/6,000 feet), the Subalpine Forest (2,440 metres/8,000 feet), and the Alpine Zone (located above the tree line at 2,900 metres/9,500 feet).[26] The Alpine Zone can only be seen up close by hiking into the high elevations of Yosemite's wilderness.

The most impressive plants in the Yosemite ecosystem are the giant sequoia trees (*Sequoiadendron giganteum*), which grow in three separate locations en route to the park: the Mariposa, Merced and Tuolumne groves. Giant sequoias are the largest trees in the world when measured by total volume; they occur naturally only in groves on the western slopes of the Sierra Nevada Mountains. They are different from giant redwoods (*Sequoia sempervirens*), which are taller in height and grow near the coast. Both species are native only to California.

Thomas A. Ayres, *The High Falls, Valley of the Yosemite, California*, June 1855, charcoal, white chalk and pencil on paper.

George Tirrell, 'The Grizzled Giant', engraving from J. M. Hutchings, *Scenes of Wonder and Curiosity in California* (1862). Better known as the 'Grizzly Giant', the tree still stands in the Mariposa Grove of giant sequoias.

On the floor of Yosemite Valley, visitors are more likely to see California black oak, ponderosa pine, incense-cedar and white fir. Red fir and lodgepole pine are typical of the Upper Montane forest, which also hosts Jeffrey pine – a tree with bark that smells like vanilla – and the picturesque western juniper trees immortalized by the photographer Edward Weston. The oldest known lodgepole pine in the United States is located in the park, just east of Tuolumne. 'Dendrologists, who took a tree-ring sample from a fire scar to minimize harm to this living tree, believe it would have germinated in the year 1381.'[27]

The giant sequoia may be the king of Yosemite flora, but nature enthusiasts find many other species of interest. At the opposite end of the scale is the little snow plant (*Sarcodes sanguinea*), which shoots up early in the spring while snow is still on the ground. John Muir described it as 'red, fleshy and watery', adding that it resembled 'a gigantic asparagus shoot'. Muir considered the snow plant Yosemite's most intriguing botanical species. 'Soon after the snow is off the ground', he wrote, it 'rises through the dead needles and humus in the pine and fir woods like a bright glowing pillar of fire'. Although admired as a curiosity, Muir noted, 'nobody loves it as lilies, violets, roses, daisies are loved.'[28]

Another Yosemite plant, the Sierra sweet bay (*Myrica hartwegii*), is noted for its rarity. Designated a 'special status' shrub, it is found in only five counties in the Sierra Nevada Mountains. At Yosemite it grows

Snow plant (*Sarcodes sanguinea*), named because it comes
up in early spring when there is still snow on the ground.

Monkeyflower (*Mimulus filicaulis*), Yosemite, a federal
'species of concern' within the park.

in two locations: on sandbars and riverbanks along the South Fork of
the Merced River downstream from Wawona, and along Big Creek.[29]
The leaves of the Sierra sweet bay have antiseptic and pain-relieving
properties.

The vegetation in Yosemite National Park contains at least 1,374
species of vascular plants in addition to bryophytes (non-vascular plants)
and lichens. Of these, 109 are listed as federal 'species of concern', have
been accorded 'rare' status by the State of California or are considered by park employees to be rare within the park.[30] Among the six
federal species of concern are the Yosemite woolly sunflower (*Eriophyllum
nubigenum*) and the slender-stemmed monkeyflower (*Mimulus filicaulis*).
Despite its name, the woolly sunflower is a short plant with small yellow
flowers, having little in common with the flowers painted by Van Gogh.
The monkeyflower, purple in colour, is another low-growing plant. More
attractive, despite its name, is the Yosemite onion (*Allium yosemitense*),
one of four state-listed rare species.

Tagged Yosemite black bear, scourge of the family minivan.

Yosemite National Park provides essential habitat for a wide variety of animal species, with 90 mammal species living inside park boundaries. Rodents, with 39 species, are the largest group of mammals in the park.[31] Tourists are most familiar with the squirrels and chipmunks that brazenly visit campsites and picnics in search of food. The California ground squirrel is the most abundant of the park's five species. There are six species of chipmunk, as well as mice, marmots, gophers, woodrats, voles, beavers and porcupines.

Considerably more intimidating are the bears that occasionally explore campgrounds in search of food. In the first half of the twentieth century campers left food unattended at campsites and even fed bears in the park, sometimes with disastrous results. As one scholar points out, an 'entire generation of park visitors' grew up with the idea that national park bears were 'not really "wild" animals'.[32] Feeding wildlife is forbidden by modern-day park management, but these animals continually surprise us. According to a recent press release, during the first decade of the twenty-first century, 'the top choice of vehicle by black bears in Yosemite National Park has been the minivan.'[33] These family vehicles are often littered with crumbs and juice boxes left by small children. An estimated 300–500 black bears now live within the park boundaries.

Yosemite's other large predator is the mountain lion (*Puma concolor*), North America's largest member of the cat family. Mountain lions are also known as cougars, pumas and panthers. Although they are occasionally seen chasing raccoons and coyotes near Yosemite's inhabited areas, they are more shy than bears and seldom interact with

Sierra Nevada bighorn sheep (*Ovis canadensis sierrae*), the only mammal on both state and federal lists of endangered species.

The beautiful but annoying Steller's jay (*Cyanocitta stelleri*)
on a manzanita branch at Mirror Lake, Yosemite.

humans. From 1907 to the 1960s the mountain lion was viewed by the State of California as a 'bountied predator' and state money was offered in an attempt to eradicate them. Their status changed to 'big game' in 1969, making them available for trophy hunting. In 1990 Californians voted to pass Proposition 117, banning almost all killing of mountain lions in the state. As a result, the number of mountain lions at Yosemite is now on the rise.[34] Smaller predators include the coyote, which is occasionally seen trotting along park roads, and a few species of weasels and skunks.

Seventeen mammals at Yosemite have been given special status by either the federal or state government. Only one, the Sierra Nevada bighorn sheep (*Ovis canadensis sierrae*), is on both federal and state lists of endangered species. The Pacific fisher (*Martes pennanti*), an animal resembling an otter, is a candidate for the list, and the Mount Lyell shrew (*Sorex lyelli*), which is native to the Yosemite region, is considered a California 'species of concern'.

In addition to the Sierra Nevada bighorn sheep, hooved mammals in the park include mule deer and feral pigs. Deer, like coyotes, are frequently seen by visitors, while the Sierra Nevada red fox and the white-tailed jackrabbit appear very rarely.[35] In January 2015, motion-sensitive cameras in the park photographed the Sierra Nevada red fox (*Vulpes vulpes necator*) on two separate occasions. One of the rarest mammals in North America, the species had not been sighted at Yosemite for nearly a century.

Over 165 species of migrating, wintering and breeding birds live at Yosemite, while another hundred species visit the park occasionally. Birdwatchers most often watch for great grey owls, spotted owls, peregrine falcons, pileated woodpeckers and northern goshawks. The species most commonly seen are the Steller's jay, American robin, acorn woodpecker, common raven and mountain chickadee.[36] The Steller's jay (*Cyanocitta stelleri*), which often steals food at picnic sites and snack bars, is probably the most annoying Yosemite avian. This beautiful blue bird symbolizes the difficulty of finding a happy balance between nature and tourism at Yosemite: an attractive species in itself, it has become a pest in the most highly populated areas of the valley.

TWO

Discovery: Weird Beauty and Terrible Grandeur

The first white Americans to see Yosemite Valley were probably those travelling with Joseph R. Walker, an Army scout and mountain man who led an expeditionary party into the Sierra Nevada mountains in 1833. Operating under orders from the explorer Captain Benjamin Bonneville, Walker and his party travelled across the Sierra on foot. One member of the party, Zenas Leonard, kept a journal of their trip that was later published. While trudging along a ridge in the mountains, the group encountered many small streams shooting 'from one lofty precipice to another', as well as rock cliffs 'more than a mile high', and a seemingly inaccessible valley.[1] Historians have identified this as a description of Yosemite Valley seen from its northern rim.

Two prospectors, William Penn Abrams and U. N. Reamer, were the second Anglo-Americans to see the valley when they entered its western end in 1849. The miners failed to publish an account of their visit, but there is no doubt they saw Yosemite. Abrams described its features in his diary: 'a valley enclosed by stupendous cliffs rising perhaps 3,000 feet from their base', a waterfall dropping 'from a cliff below three jagged peaks', and 'a rounded mountain . . . which looked as though it has been sliced with a knife as one would slice a loaf of bread'.[2] Abrams perfectly described the walls of Yosemite Valley and the formations known today as Bridalveil Falls, Cathedral Rocks and Half Dome.

It was not until 1851 that news of Yosemite began to spread throughout California. That was the year Major James D. Savage and the Mariposa Battalion pursued a band of Native Americans into Yosemite after skirmishes in the area.[3] The story of the Mariposa Battalion was recorded by Lafayette Houghton Bunnell, a member of the group, who wrote that during 1850 the natives in Mariposa County 'became very troublesome to the miners and settlers'.[4]

One incident involved Savage, who was then working as a trader and miner near the mouth of the South Fork of the Merced River, some 15 miles below Yosemite. In early 1850 Savage's trading post and mining camp were attacked by a band of natives. The California state militia established a unit called the Mariposa Battalion to take control of the situation. Savage, who had fought in the Mexican–American War, was placed in charge. He was something of a character, having 'gone native' by marrying five indigenous women in his efforts to establish friendly ties with tribes in the area.

Pursuing a band of Native Americans into the mountains, Savage and his men found themselves looking out over Yosemite Valley from a vantage point along the trail. Afterwards, they told stories of their adventure throughout the state and received credit for 'discovering' the valley. The Mariposa Battalion also proposed the name 'Yosemite', then believed to be a 'beautiful and sonorous corruption of the word for "grizzly bear"'.[5]

The early history of the valley is also intertwined with the story of James Mason Hutchings, the Yosemite settler, innkeeper and self-proclaimed publicist of the valley. An English immigrant, Hutchings arrived in California during the Gold Rush of 1849. Although successful as a miner, he went bankrupt twice – the first time because his bank failed, the second because he had invested unwisely in an ill-fated canal-building project.[6] Turning to journalism, Hutchings began as a writer and substitute editor for the *Placerville Herald*, the newspaper of a mining town in the Sierra Nevada foothills. He also designed a series of illustrated letter sheets (a form of poster printed on paper). 'The Miner's Ten Commandments', published in 1853, was a best-selling letter sheet and convinced Hutchings that images and news of California could prove lucrative.

Described by an acquaintance as 'an enthusiast, a dreamer, a visionary',[7] Hutchings organized the earliest thoroughly documented 'tourist excursion' to Yosemite. (Another group had visited the previous year, but no detailed record of their trip has been found.) Hutchings conceived the notion of bringing an artist along to help chronicle his excursion of 1855. Many who had heard the early reports about Yosemite assumed they were 'tall tales', and early estimates of the size of its cliffs and

waterfalls were considered exaggerations. Hutchings hoped to witness Yosemite's amazing scenery himself and provide visual proof of what he saw.

In San Francisco he visited a draftsman named Thomas A. Ayres, who had arrived in California with the Gold Rush. After experiencing the hardships of life as a miner, Ayres returned to painting, but found

George Tirrell, *View of Sacramento, California, from Across the Bay,*
c. 1855, oil on canvas.

that career equally challenging on the frontier. Hutchings commented sympathetically that Ayres felt discouraged about his life as an artist in San Francisco, noting that 'all he makes for one picture is spent before he gets an order for another.'[8] San Francisco did not yet have a large art market, nor was Ayres the best painter working there.

In those days, Yosemite-bound visitors travelled by steamboat from the city of Oakland, located across the bay from San Francisco; heading upriver, they usually went to Stockton overnight, a ride made less pleasant by mosquitoes. The next portion of the journey involved a series of stagecoach rides with overnight stops at small towns in California's central valley and the Sierra Nevada foothills.[9] Travelling by stagecoach was a notoriously dusty, tiring mode of travel. The final leg of the journey took place on horseback, along one of three trails into the valley: the Big Oak Flat and Coulterville trails from the west, and the Mariposa Trail from the southwest via Wawona.

Hutchings, Ayres and Hutchings's friend Walter Millard of San Francisco took the steamship *Martin White* to Sacramento on 5 July 1855, and continued from there by stagecoach. On the way they visited the Calaveras Grove of giant sequoias – 'mammoth vegetable-giants', as Hutchings called them. The sightseers named most of the trees in the grove.[10] Later that year Hutchings published a print, 'The Mammoth Tree Grove', using sketches Ayres made during their visit.

Hutchings's party arrived at Yosemite Valley on 27 July. They spent two days sightseeing, with Ayres sketching the scenery, then left on 30 July to begin the long return trip.[11] Ayres's first sketch of the valley was *General View of the Yo-ham-i-te Valley*, a panoramic view from the

'Valley of the Yosemite, California', engraving based on a drawing of 1855 by Thomas A. Ayres from Mrs H. J. Taylor's *Yosemite Indians and Other Sketches* (1936).

Charles L. Weed, *Mirror Lake and Reflections, Yo-Semite Valley*, 1864, albumen photograph from Weed's second trip to the valley.

Mariposa Trail as it enters the southwest end of the valley. The view from this famous spot, which soon became known as Inspiration Point, encompasses El Capitan on the left, Bridalveil Fall on the right and Half Dome in the distance. The precise location of Inspiration Point has shifted over the years, but its present home is at the end of the Wawona tunnel, where many modern-day visitors take their first photos of the valley. Tour buses and cars stop and disgorge thousands of shutterbugs every year.

Ayres's charming albeit amateurish pencil and charcoal drawings were the first pictorial representations of the valley. They were widely disseminated to the public in print form, providing substantiation of Hutchings's claims about Yosemite scenery. Hutchings published the story of their travels in a periodical, *Hutchings' California Magazine*, which he introduced in 1856. An article in the first issue, dated July 1856, was illustrated with four of Ayres's drawings. Hutchings also published individual, large-format lithographs of the two most iconic

Photographer's First Glimpse of the Yo Semite Valley, California (Charles L. Pond and his Stereoscopic Camera), 1871, albumen stereograph taken by Martin Mason Hazeltine and published by Charles L. Pond.

images: *The Yo-ham-i-te Falls* was printed in the autumn of 1855 and *General View of the Yo-ham-i-te Valley* appeared in 1859.

Four years later, Hutchings invited Charles L. Weed to capture Yosemite's scenery in photographic form. Where Ayres's drawings had left room for questions, it must have seemed that photographs – given their reputation for verisimilitude – would dispel any lingering doubts about the veracity of reports concerning the valley. As a tourist of 1859 noted, 'Ayres' drawings are truthful, but do not approach to giving an idea of this wonderful Valley.'[12] As a 'mirror of reality', photographs were needed to establish its credibility.

Weed learned his craft as a 'camera operator', employed first at George W. Watson's Daguerreian gallery in Sacramento and then at Robert H. Vance's San Francisco studio. Vance sponsored Weed's first trip to Yosemite. After his return the San Francisco *Daily Times* announced that 'Mr C. L. Weed ... has just returned from a visit to the Yosemite Valley where he took, for Mr Vance, some forty stereoscopic views of that celebrated locality.'[13] Stereoscopic views are pairs of images, mounted side by side, that simulate depth when seen through a stereopticon viewer. Weed also took a series of about twenty 25.4 × 35.6-cm (10 × 14-inch) negatives that he printed using the salted paper process.

A photograph taken in 1871 gives modern viewers a sense of the difficulty photographers faced in getting their equipment into the mountains. Taken by Martin Mason Hazeltine, it shows Hazeltine's colleague Charles L. Pond riding a mule into Yosemite with a case of supplies strapped to his back and his binocular camera and tripod over his shoulder. The collodion wet-plate process, used by most early Yosemite photographers after Weed's first series of salt prints, involved cumbersome large cameras, tripods and glass-plate negatives that were carted around with great difficulty. The photographers had to prepare their glass negatives on site with collodion (gun cotton dissolved in alcohol and ether), followed by a mixture of potassium iodide and potassium bromide. The negatives required developing immediately after exposure, while still wet – hence the designation 'wet-plate photography'.[14]

Bringing photographic supplies into the wilderness was a challenge, as another photographer, Ellwood A. Garrett, discovered during his visit of 1871. According to a colleague, Garrett got his 'traps' and 'big photo tent' into the valley successfully. But when his pack-train mule began to ford the river at night, the beast 'was carried down the stream . . . rolled over with all the photo traps, and was drowned . . . All his things were soaking wet. His plates were all albumenized' and ruined. Another visiting photographer gave Garrett half a pound of negative collodion, which allowed him to resume his work.[15]

Hutchings, who had invited both Ayres and Weed to Yosemite, was an interesting character. In 1860 – the year after his excursion with Weed – he married a delicate, dreamy young woman named Elvira Sproat, who was 22 years his junior. In 1864 Mr and Mrs Hutchings took over an existing structure in the valley called the Upper Hotel and renamed it Hutchings' Hotel. Elvira's mother, who moved in with them, was Hutchings's 'true business partner' as well as the hotel's chief cook and housekeeper.[16] According to many tourist accounts, Hutchings was more interested in talking with his patrons than in serving hot meals on time. The travel writer Helen Hunt Jackson said of him, 'Artistic sensibility and enthusiasm do not help a man to order dinner.'[17]

Hutchings's hotel was notorious for the sheets of cloth that served as walls between guest rooms and the wide cracks between floor and wall. One of the most entertaining descriptions of the hotel was written by a visitor named Callie, whose account appeared in the *Union County Herald*:

Lawrence & Houseworth, *Hutchings' Hotel, Yosemite Valley*,
c. 1870, half of an albumen stereograph.

Upstairs the rooms were only divided by pieces of cotton cloth, and were very small at that, containing a small bed, a small rough wash-stand, a rough bench, and no place to hang anything. The only choice being to go to bed with one's clothes on, or leave them under the bed, on the floor. Of course every word and movement were very audible, and it required some little strategy to place the candle so that one's figure should not appear on the cloth partition, hugely magnified, for the amusement of one's neighbors. Fanny J's soap slipped from her fingers when washing, and flew down into the parlor, because the floor and the outside wall didn't quite meet.[18]

Hutchings' Hotel was also known for its 'Big Tree Room', a kitchen with an enormous cedar tree growing through the roof, which Hutchings had refused to cut down when the room was added. His mother-in-law hung pots and pans from nails hammered into its trunk.

Hutchings and his wife had three children. The first was Florence, nicknamed 'Floy', who was born in 1864 and celebrated locally as the first white child born in the valley. Floy was widely known among residents and tourists as a tomboy with a personality rivalling her father's. John Muir admired her free-spirited ways, and the photographer Eadweard Muybridge is said to have taught her to say, when she was only a toddler, 'I used to smoke a meerschaum, but now I smoke a "torn tob"'(a corncob pipe).[19] Floy died at the age of seventeen in a mountain-climbing accident. A second daughter, Gertrude (nicknamed 'Cosie'), was born in 1867, and a son, William Mason Hutchings, followed in 1869.

Hutchings was dismayed when Yosemite Valley was declared a state park only six weeks after he and his family took up innkeeping. His fear that his property rights would be jeopardized by the valley's park status was realized, and the Yosemite Commissioners attempted to force him and another early homesteader, James C. Lamon, out of the valley. When the dispute was taken to court, the homesteaders lost and were forced to give up their claims to the land. Hutchings fought

George Fiske, *Big Tree Room, Barnard's Hotel* [formerly Hutchings' Hotel], *Yosemite, c.* 1884, albumen photograph.

eviction for twelve years, finally leaving the valley in 1875. His wife Elvira divorced him the same year, but he soon met a young widow named Augusta Ladd Sweetland and married her in 1879. Hutchings, his children and his second wife wintered in San Francisco, returning to Yosemite every summer. Hutchings would make his final visit to the valley in 1902, accompanied by his third wife. When one of the horses took fright he was thrown from his carriage, fractured his skull and died by the roadside.

The many articles about Yosemite published by Hutchings and others achieved their intended goal: to entice more visitors to California and Yosemite. Tourist numbers increased markedly after completion of the transatlantic railroad in 1869. The overland journey from the East Coast, which had previously taken weeks or even months, could be managed in only six days. Even Yosemite, in its remote mountain fastness, began to show signs of civilization. The painter James D. Smillie, who dreamed of painting wilderness scenery when he went there in 1871, complained about the changes he found: 'I had hoped that here, at last, I had got away from modern improvements, Rail Roads, & Telegraphs, but last night the very evening we arrived, a telegraph

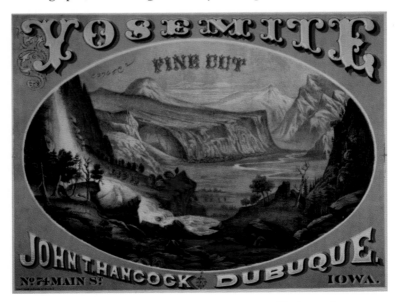

Yosemite Fine Cut, tobacco label for John T. Hancock of Dubuque, Iowa, 1872.

Platter in 'Yosemite' transferware pattern, 1883, T. & R. Boote pottery, Staffordshire.

wire was brought into the valley & communications completed. I find also a saloon with velvet carpets, two billiard tables, etc. etc.'[20]

By 1869 Yosemite was well on its way to becoming a popular vacation destination. Only a handful of tourists came to the valley during the first few years; by the 1860s the annual count still numbered only in the hundreds. According to one source, tourist totals nearly doubled after completion of the transatlantic railroad: 623 visitors came in 1868; 1,122 arrived the following year.[21] Although these numbers appear small compared with the millions who visit today, they seemed large enough in 1872 for the geologist Josiah D. Whitney to warn a friend against going to Yosemite until the 'rush' of summer visitors had passed.[22]

Barely two decades after its discovery, the name 'Yosemite' conveyed such panache that household products were named for it. An Ohio firm copyrighted a label for 'Yosemite Fine Cut Tobacco' in 1872. (The image, which depicts a view from the base of Upper Yosemite Falls, was reused by other tobacconists, including John T. Hancock of Iowa.) A dry goods manufacturer in New York registered the name 'Yosemite Mills' two years later.[23] In the 1880s T. & R. Boote, an English pottery near Stoke-on-Trent, Staffordshire, registered a trademark for a 'Yosemite' pattern. Large platters were decorated with an image of a fallen sequoia tree, but cups and smaller plates exhibit nothing related to Yosemite other than the name on the bottom. These marketing ploys took advantage of the fact that Yosemite was an exotic and memorable name, despite its lacking any connections to tobacco, dry goods or china.

By the 1870s Yosemite was one of the country's most famous tourist destinations. Many visitors would have agreed with a tourist named Herbert Aulls, who wrote an account of his visit of 1876. Aulls noted that of all he had seen on his travels, he was most impressed by the 'weird Beauty and terrible Grandeur' of the 'towering, tottering cliffs over Yo-Semite'.[24]

THREE

Yosemite as Home

Yosemite Valley was occupied by Native Americans for thousands of years before white immigrants first saw it in the 1850s. When increasing numbers of Anglo-Americans began to arrive in the mid-nineteenth century, the people most closely associated with the valley were the Miwok of the Sierra Nevada region and a local group called the Ahwahneechee, who had lived in or near Yosemite for at least 600 years. Related to the Northern Paiute and Mono groups, the Ahwahneechee may have descended from indigenous people who settled in the valley around 3,000 years ago, or they may have replaced those earlier inhabitants around 1100 to 1400 CE.[1] Although a small number of indigenous people may have wintered in the valley, most spent the harsh Sierra winters at lower elevations along the Merced and Tuolumne Rivers.

Linguists subdivide the Miwok of the Sierra Nevada mountains and foothills into the Northern, Central and Southern Miwok. East of Yosemite were the Paiutes; north of Yosemite, in Carson Valley and nearby, were the Washoe. To the south and west were the Northern Valley Yokuts; and southeast of Yosemite, around the headwaters of the Kings and San Joaquin Rivers, were the Western Mono.[2] Descendants of these groups still live in roughly the same locations.

The Native Americans at Yosemite developed their own mythology to explain the creation of the valley's imposing rock formations. Their beliefs remained an oral tradition until white Americans, including James Mason Hutchings and Galen Clark, began to put them on paper. Poetic and highly romanticized, these indigenous stories were likely transcribed with errors by the Anglo-Americans who first wrote them down. Clark, whose book *Indians of the Yosemite Valley and Vicinity* (1904) includes a chapter on myths and legends, noted that it was extremely difficult to get reliable information because the indigenous people were reluctant to speak of their beliefs.[3]

Hutchings, who published a charming myth about Half Dome and El Capitan in his *California Magazine* in 1859, almost certainly fabricated most of it.[4] His account of the Ahwahneechee myth characterizes El Capitan as the seat of a proud male spirit named Tu-toch-ah-nu-lah and Half Dome as the seat of a beautiful female spirit named Tes-sa-ach. One morning, Tu-toch-ah-nu-lah saw the lovely Tes-sa-ach sitting on Half Dome; after calling his name, she disappeared over the rounded top of the dome. Every day Tu-toch-ah-nu-lah searched for the lovely maiden without success. 'So strong was his thought of her that he forgot the crops of Yo-Semite, and they, without rain, wanting his tender care, quickly drooped their heads and shrunk. The wind whistled mournfully through the wild corn, the wild bee stored no more honey in the hollow tree . . . and the green leaves became brown.'

Tes-sa-ach 'looked with sorrowing eyes over the neglected valley' and called upon the Great Spirit to revive its 'bright flowers and delicate grasses, green trees, and nodding acorns'. With an awful crashing sound,

Martin Mason Hazeltine, *Miwok Village, Yosemite*,
with burden baskets in foreground and conical wooden
shelters in background, *c*. 1870, half of an albumen stereograph.

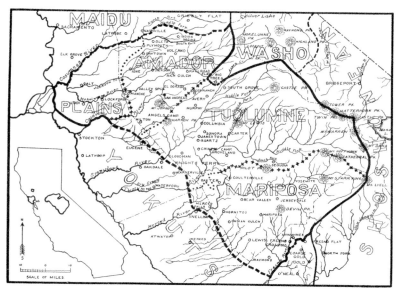

Samuel Alfred Barrett, 'Map of Miwok Groups in the Yosemite Area', 1908.

'the dome of granite opened beneath her feet', and life returned to the valley. Tes-sa-ach disappeared, never to be seen again. 'Yet, that all might hold her memory in their hearts, she left the quiet lake, the winding river, and yonder half-dome, which still bears her name.' Tu-toch-ah-nu-lah, in turn, carved his own profile on the face of El Capitan, 'that the Yo-Semites might never forget him'.[5]

A more reputable source provides a different creation myth for Half Dome. In this version, an indigenous woman named Tes-sa-ach and her husband travelled a great distance to reach the valley. The woman, walking ahead of her husband and bending forward 'under the heavy burden of her great conical basket', reached the valley first and drank all the water in the lake, causing a great drought. Her actions angered her husband, who beat her with his staff. She wept and became angry, scolding him and throwing her basket at him. 'At the very moment that they stood facing each other, the woman and her husband were turned into stone for their wickedness. There they have remained to this day. The basket lies upturned beside the husband, and the woman's rock face is stained with the long, dark lines from her tears.'[6] The husband and the burden basket became North Dome and Basket Dome, both located

Daniel San Souci, 'Two Bear Cubs', watercolour, from Robert San Souci's book
Two Bear Cubs: A Miwok Legend from California's Yosemite Valley (1997).

on the north side of Yosemite; the woman became Half Dome, across the valley to the south.

The same reputable source provides an interesting creation legend for El Capitan. In this story, two bear cubs living in Ah-wah'-nee splashed and played in the river, wearing themselves out. They climbed a huge boulder and lay down to rest, but their exhausted sleep lasted 'moons and snows, both winter and summer'. During their long sleep, the boulder that held them began to rise slowly 'until it had lifted them high into the sky'. The birds and animals of Ah-wah'-nee missed the cubs and came to help them, but none could jump or climb high enough to reach the clifftop. It was Tu-toch-ah-nu-lah, the lowly 'measuring worm', who finally climbed El Capitan and carried the cubs back down to the valley. The cliff was named in his honour.[7]

The lives of the indigenous people, as documented by nineteenth-century Anglo-American writers, offer a window onto the more distant past. Yosemite provided plentiful food during the warm months; acorns, available in the autumn, were a dietary staple. Other foods included Manzanita berries, bulbs, corms (a form of root related to bulbs and rhizomes), mushrooms, deer, squirrel and fish. One writer noted that 'deer meat was the most highly regarded flesh, with the meat of the California Gray Squirrel a close second.' Seeds were considered 'luxuries' and acorns 'the finest vegetable food'. The individual with plenty of acorns and venison was considered 'well off'.[8] Bulbs and corms – sometimes called 'wild potatoes' – were dug up with a long stick, a practice that caused early Anglo-American travellers to call the Miwok 'Digger Indians', although that appellation has long been considered derogatory.

Acorn soup was made by most indigenous groups in central California, including those at Yosemite, and its preparation was a complicated process. Acorns are rich in nutrition but bitter because they contain tannin, so preparing them required leaching out the tannin. The acorns were first cracked open and the nuts removed from their hard outer shells and soft inner linings. Next they were pounded into flour with a stone pestle against depressions in outcroppings of local bedrock. Many of these bedrock 'mortars' are still visible in Yosemite and the surrounding area.

At this point the acorn flour was ready for cooking. Surprisingly the indigenous people used tightly woven baskets for cooking: they dropped hot stones, preheated in a fire, directly into a mixture of water and acorn flour. The resulting soup was stirred constantly to avoid having the hot stones burn either the basket or the food. Acorn flour was cooked as soup or processed further into moist, semi-solid forms resembling biscuits and bread, which were baked in earth ovens.[9]

As shown in early photographs and paintings, the Miwok lived in conical, above-ground houses called *umachas* that were made with slabs of bark. They created a variety of other structures including semi-subterranean conical dwelling houses, assembly houses likewise built partially underground, rectangular ceremonial structures made of brush, grinding booths, acorn granaries, sun shelters and hunting blinds made of green boughs, from which they shot birds and animals. The acorn granaries or *chuk'kas* were made with thatched pine branches, the needles pointing downward to keep out mice and squirrels as well as snow and rain. The Miwok even built sweat-houses, which were heated by fire rather than steam; their purpose was to induce sweating in men and boys for relaxation and curative purposes.[10]

Because they stayed at Yosemite during the warm months, indigenous men wore only a deerskin breech-cloth, 'either draped about the loins or passed between the legs'. Women wore a 'knee-length double apron of deerskin, fringed, and beaded on the fringe, or a loin-cloth like that of the men'. In cooler weather, both men and women wore a small

Bedrock Mortars at Chaw'se Indian Grinding Rock
State Historic Park, northwest of Yosemite.

Charles C. Pierce, *Paiute Indian Acorn Caches
or Granaries in Yosemite Valley, c. 1902.*

cape of deer fur or woven rabbit skins around their shoulders. Deerskin
moccasins were also a necessity in cold weather.[11]

The Miwoks' conical huts, their 'burden baskets' and their elevated
storage bins called *chukahs* were documented by many nineteenth-
century writers, painters and photographers. Most painters included
Native Americans as a focal point and a bit of colour, rather than for
ethnographic reasons. Lady Constance Gordon-Cumming was one

Raymond D. Yelland, *Yosemite Indian Village*, 1874, oil on canvas.
The natives' shelters were called *umachas*.

of the only painters who focused on the indigenous people for their
own sake. Gordon-Cumming's painting of a Miwok camp with Half
Dome in the background includes wooden dwellings, acorn granaries
and infant carriers. Two women are shown pounding acorns in natural
stone mortars; another is placing a heated stone into a basket to cook
the ingredients; and animal pelts hang above them in trees.

Early Yosemite photographers were more interested than the
painters in documenting the valley's original inhabitants for ethnographic and educational reasons. Their interest had a commercial component: the more variety in their stereographs and other photos, the
more sales they could make to tourists and armchair travellers back east.
In retrospect some of these images seem quite patronizing. John James
Reilly's stereograph of several Miwok women and children shows a group
of bedraggled individuals who appear to be living a near-subsistence
lifestyle. Many white tourists had trouble seeing beyond the long hair
and mismatched clothing of the indigenous people. These photographs
reference the racial stereotyping that so often went hand in hand with
attitudes of imperialism.

Other nineteenth-century photographs make a poignant statement
about the diminishing status of Yosemite's indigenous people. Julius

Boysen's *Yo-Chak, Yosemite*, taken in 1900, shows an elderly man standing alone in the valley with Cathedral Rocks as a backdrop; he is thin and his clothing is somewhat tattered but he stands upright, seemingly proud, if alone. A photograph by Gustav Fagersteen titled *The Last One of the Yosemite Tribe* depicts a seated white-haired man who is presumably the last surviving member of his group. These images go beyond portraiture. By including so much landscape around the figures, the photographers have heightened the sense of isolation and loneliness their images convey.

Following the Gold Rush of 1849, Native Americans in the Sierra Nevada region were forced to give up their hunting and gathering lifestyle. As one writer explains, 'The massive invasion of miners who poured over the mountains brutally displaced entire native communities, while the environmental destruction wrought by mining practices undermined seasonal hunting and gathering cycles.'[12] Some indigenous people moved farther away from mining areas; others found employment at the margins of white society.

Those who remained in Yosemite Valley found employment in the new culture of commerce that developed in tandem with tourism. Many were hired to work at the hotels and other businesses located in the

Constance Gordon-Cumming, *Indian Camp Beside the Merced River with North and South Domes*, 1878, watercolour on paper.

valley. Galen Clark noted in the 1890s that young women 'find it easier
to make money by washing and sewing or almost any other [domestic]
work'. Indigenous men found employment chopping wood, harvesting
hay, labouring for hotels, serving as guides, driving wagons and selling
fish and game to tourists and hotels. One scholar has noted that, at
first, working as domestics and labourers supplemented the indigenous
people's traditional lifestyle; eventually it replaced it entirely.[13]

White Americans held a variety of attitudes toward Yosemite's
indigenous inhabitants. Gordon-Cumming noted that an 'Indian gipsy
camp' in the valley inspired heated debates during her visit of 1878.
Some considered the Native Americans 'a race of scoundrels', while
others saw them more sympathetically as 'a race unjustly despoiled of
their heritage'.[14] With condescending comments about their cleanliness
and the derogatory expression 'Digger Indians' in common use, it is
heartening to learn that some Anglo-Americans were sympathetic to
the indigenous population even in the nineteenth century.

The historian Frederick Turner noted in his much-publicized
'frontier thesis' that by 1890, there was no longer an American frontier.[15]
White settlements stretched across the entire continent and Native
Americans were relegated almost entirely to reservations. California was
no longer the domain of desperadoes and 'wild Indians'. A more recent
historian has expanded on this theme: 'The 1890s thus dawned nostalgic
and the hard-won West began to take on the aura of a romantic journey.
Whereas Indians had been considered savages and warriors in the
recent past, they were now symbols of the Frontier and understood to
be heroes.'[16]

By the end of the century, a growing number of Western Mono and
Mono Lake Paiutes were visiting Yosemite. Many stayed in the valley
three or four weeks gathering acorns, then left by the Yosemite Falls
Trail. Miwok and Chukchansi Yokuts also came to the valley. In 1903
the writer George Wharton James noted that 'The Yosemite Indians
of to-day are generally either Paiutis [sic] or Monos.'[17] Julia Parker, a
modern-day Yosemite resident of Kashia Pomo ancestry, considers her
peers a mix of Paiute and Miwok.[18]

Yosemite's indigenous inhabitants were in a sense 'commodified' as
part of the tourist experience. A woman known as Indian Mary spent
much of her adult life in the valley. By the early twentieth century, she

Julius Boysen, *Yo-Chak, Yosemite*, 1900. By including a lot of landscape around the figure, Boysen heightened the sense of isolation.

Basket weavers Tina Charlie, Carrie Bethel, Alice Wilson,
Leanna Tom and Maggie Howard with chief park ranger
Forest Townsley at an 'Indian Field Day', Yosemite, 1925.

lived in a small cabin at the base of Sentinel Rock and made a living
selling her baskets and posing for photographs.[19] Native Americans were
also featured during Indian Field Days, a series of events held in the
valley between 1916 and 1929. The Indian Field Days were conceived
and managed by the Desmond Park Company, forerunner of the
Yosemite National Park Company. Indigenous peoples in the area were
invited to a barbecue in the valley; in return they were paid to entertain
visiting tourists with dances, horse races and craft displays.

Because the first Indian Field Day in 1916 was less successful than
its organizers had hoped, the second was not held until 1920, when it
became a 'full-fledged rodeo complete with horse-bucking, pony races,
and mounted tugs-of-war'.[20] Later versions were cut back from three-
day events to two, but the number of tourists and indigenous participants
continued to increase. Indian Field Days were endorsed by the National
Park Service as a means of increasing tourism, but they had little to do
with the daily life of the indigenous people. They were events designed
for tourist entertainment, like the Yosemite Firefall, the Glacier Point
Chicken Toss and the Bracebridge Dinner so beloved of Ansel Adams
(see chapter Seven). The Firefall occurred when glowing coals were

poured off Glacier Point Cliff at night; in the Chicken Toss, a live chicken was thrown from the cliff, survived the drop and walked back to its clifftop home by evening.[21]

For the Indian Field Days of 1929, indigenous men who 'stripped and painted as warriors' were paid $2 for the two days. Those wearing 'their own costumes' were paid $5, as long as their clothing met the requirements of the judges: 'war bonnet or feather headdress; buckskin jacket, pants and moccasins or buckskin dress and moccasins'. Special events included Indian ceremonial dances and war dances, and a half-day was devoted to the exhibition, judging and sale of Indian baskets and beadwork, with collectors from San Francisco and other cities invited to attend.[22]

Hazel Hogan, an eighteen-year-old Mono Lake Paiute, was crowned Miss Yosemite and Queen of the Indian Days Celebration in 1929. Although admired as the most beautiful young indigenous woman, Hogan was considered insufficiently 'native' in appearance when she appeared in a modern 'marcelled' haircut.[23] As shown in photographs, a white hairband covered the problematic hairdo. Despite her obvious beauty, Miss Hogan required the proper 'packaging' to be considered an appropriate Queen of the Indian Field Days. In addition to being a local beauty, she was a talented craftswoman whose beaded belt was exhibited at the California State Fair in 1929 and afterwards sent as a gift to the American First Lady, Mrs Herbert Hoover.

Apart from the Indian Field Days, indigenous women gave casual demonstrations of basket making, acorn pounding, cooking and other subsistence activities, providing tourists with an informal educational experience. After the construction of the Yosemite Museum in 1926, those demonstrations became more formalized under the auspices of the National Park Service. A few local women, most of them Paiute in ancestry, were hired by the Park Service to demonstrate basket making and cooking techniques.[24]

In the early 1930s a simulated Indian Village, complete with conical bark shelters and acorn *chuk'kas*, was constructed behind the Yosemite Museum. This early village was made more permanent in the 1970s with the addition of a round house, a wooden cabin and a sweat-house constructed partially underground.[25] The so-called 'Indian Village of Ahwahnee' remains to this day.

Maggie Howard, a Mono Lake Paiute, was one of the first indigenous women to demonstrate acorn preparation and basket weaving at the Indian Village. She worked there from 1929 to 1942 and was succeeded in the position by Lucy Telles (the mother of Hazel Hogan), who demonstrated basket making techniques to visitors until her death in 1955. Lucy's sister Alice Wilson also earned money demonstrating basketry and selling her work to visitors. Women such as Howard, Telles and Wilson must have appreciated the income such work brought them, but 'living displays' of this sort seem rather patronizing today. While paying homage to the culture of Yosemite's early inhabitants, these displays tamed and commodified the indigenous culture, making it 'safe' for tourist consumption.

Today woven baskets are considered the indigenous people's most impressive art form.[26] Native American basketry in California was highly varied, as might be expected of a region with about 500 indigenous communities speaking 80 mutually unintelligible languages. California supported one of the most dense native populations in North America outside Mexico. Yosemite's indigenous people evolved a wide variety of basket types long before Anglo-American settlers arrived.

Maggie Howard preparing acorns, a staple of the native diet, 1936.

Baskets from the Yosemite Museum including three cradle baskets
and a large conical 'burden' basket.

Traditional basketry ranged from the conical 'burden' basket used
for gathering acorns, with its strap worn around the bearer's forehead,
to cradles in which mothers carried infants 'papoose style'. Burden baskets
were made less permeable with the addition of a paste made from cooked
bulbs of the soaproot plant (genus *Chlorogalum*); this kept seeds from
working their way through small openings in the basket. Some infant
carriers had sunshades or bonnets to protect the babies' faces from the
sun and to keep them from getting hurt if the cradle tipped over.

The Miwok created small baskets for dipping, larger baskets for
cooking and flat-bottomed baskets for general storage and serving food.
Long baskets with handles were created as 'seed beaters', used in the
process of harvesting seeds. Other long, flat, coiled baskets were used
for winnowing grain and 'parching' seeds. Edward Curtis, a celebrated
photographer of the American West, explained that 'meal or seeds were
parched by shaking them with intermixed embers'.[27] The Miwok even
made loosely woven rackets that resemble jai-alai or lacrosse sticks; both
men and women used them to play games using wooden balls.

By the 1890s collecting native baskets had reached the level of
an obsession. The writer Charles E. Holder remarked in 1891 that 'the
latest fad or craze in California . . . is to possess a collection of Indian

baskets.' Holder noted that 'some of the most artistic homes in the state have rooms decorated with them.'[28] Baskets were collected for a variety of reasons, but the most common was for decoration – to give one's home an attractive appearance. As shown in contemporary photographs, Yosemite artists likewise placed baskets artfully around their studios and homes to appeal to tourists.

Basket collections became tourist attractions in their own right. According to *Foley's Yosemite Souvenir and Guide* from around 1901–5, visitors 'will find a large collection of Indian baskets at the residence of Mr and Mrs C. B. Atkinson, opposite the guardian's office. Mrs Atkinson is an untiring collector of the basket work of the Yosemite and Paiute Indians.'[29] Mr Atkinson, who initially came to Yosemite as an employee of James Mason Hutchings, worked for the state-administered Yosemite Valley Commission.

When a basket woven by Lucy Telles won first prize at the World's Fair in Chicago in 1933, it must have seemed as if Yosemite craftsmen had reached a pinnacle of success. The basket, which was 91 cm (36 in.) in diameter, 51 cm (20 in.) high and decorated with geometric patterns, took three years to make. After its display at the World's Fair, it was exhibited at the Golden Gate International Exposition in 1939. Telles's big basket became famous. According to one source, 'postcards were sold featuring Telles and her basket, children were photographed inside it, and Ripley, of *Believe It or Not!* fame, wanted to add the basket to his collection of world curiosities.'[30]

In the 1920s and '30s the demand for baskets made by women such as Lucy Telles, Carrie Bethel and Maggie Howard turned these indigenous women into local celebrities. They continued to live humble, even impoverished private lives, however, and it seems unlikely they considered themselves 'fine artists'. As one expert notes, 'Telles was a housewife and grandmother who rose before dawn to cook breakfast for her husband, did the laundry, took care of the grandchildren, and prepared dinner.'[31] Carrie Bethel, who sold many of her baskets to the collector James Schwabacher, worked in a variety of domestic jobs: she did laundry at Tioga Lodge near Mono Lake, cooked for road crews and worked as a seasonal field labourer in the San Joaquin Valley. Ellen Amos, a basket maker who lived near Wawona, worked in the laundry of the Wawona Hotel.

Julius Boysen, *Suzie McGowan with her Daughter Sadie in a Cradleboard*
(Yosemite Falls in Background), *c.* 1901.

Julius Boysen, *Lucy Telles, also known as Pa-ma-has (1885–1955), Seated beside her Largest Basket, Completed in 1933 after about Three Years of Work, Yosemite*, 1933, gelatin silver print.

By the 1930s most of the indigenous men and women living in the valley year-round were employed by local residents, the Yosemite Park and Curry Company or the National Park Service. Most of the men worked as labourers on road crews, with a few employed as cowboys and guides to provide 'local colour' for tourists. Women continued to work as kitchen helpers, housekeepers and chambermaids in hotels.

It is hardly surprising that the relationship between park management and the indigenous people was sometimes strained. In 1932–3 the National Park Service provided their indigenous employees with thirteen new three-room cabins and two new six-room cabins, all of them furnished with cold water and located near a central shower and toilet facility. The old residential village was demolished, and Park Service officials decided which individuals would be allowed to live in the new cabins. As scholars have noted, 'For the first time Yosemite Indian people did not have a village environment of their own choosing and were obliged to pay rent.'[32]

In recent decades a few indigenous women have gained respect and employment by reviving their traditional arts. The best-known example is Julia Domingues Parker, a woman of Kashia Pomo ancestry who married a Miwok/Paiute man named Ralph Parker. (Parker was the grandson of Lucy Telles.) In 1948 Julia Parker began learning the basketry techniques practiced by her husband's family; she has been giving demonstrations of the craft ever since. Jim Snyder, former Yosemite park historian, enjoys telling a story about Parker's cooking demonstrations: 'I've seen her explaining to a little kid, "I don't stand on your kitchen table, so you shouldn't walk on my pounding rock."'

Now in her eighties, Parker is the longest-tenured park employee at Yosemite, having given cultural demonstrations for over 40 years. Although not originally native to the area, she receives the respect that eluded Yosemite's original inhabitants. According to a park spokesman, 'Julia is truly a national treasure . . . She's been honored by universities, she has baskets all over the country, she's consulted with museums.'[33] In 1983 Parker presented Great Britain's Queen Elizabeth II – then visiting Yosemite – with a basket representing a year's work. Julia Parker and others like her have worked to keep their indigenous culture alive and flourishing.

FOUR

American Eden

Many surviving travel accounts suggest that Yosemite's early Anglo-American visitors found their encounter with the valley a deeply religious experience. Seven miles (11 kilometres) long and less than a mile in width, with steep grey walls and formations resembling Gothic spires and cathedral domes, the valley was often described as a 'cathedral of nature' and the 'grandest of all Nature's temples'. Its many unusual formations led some to call it the workshop of God, the 'great sculptor'. Descriptions like these evoke the pantheistic form of Christianity exemplified by writers like John Muir, which still has many adherents in modern-day California.

Yosemite's geologic formations suggested cathedral architecture in a very literal way. The geologist Clarence King found Cathedral Rocks 'quite suggestive of the Florence Duomo' (the dome of the cathedral in Florence, Italy).[1] A Connecticut tourist of 1866 saw 'spires & towers in Gothic shapes' that reminded him of 'old ruins of Castles & Cathedrals'. Entering this 'temple of nature' at nightfall, he was inspired to remark: 'No spot on the wide earth reveals within so small a compass such marvellous [sic] handiwork of the Deity – No place can so religiously impress one.' On Sunday the same visitor 'worshipped in a temple not made with hands, but, in God's own Temple of Nature'.[2]

The Big Tree groves also evoked great natural cathedrals and thoughts of the divine. When a young female visitor from San Francisco saw the Big Trees in 1858 she exclaimed, 'Wonderful are thy works, O Lord!' Pondering their existence, she continued, 'One cannot help a feeling of awe in wandering among those majestic trees. Why are they there in that particular place? Did not some of the sons of Noah emigrate to California and plant them there? Or perhaps that locality was not reached by the flood.'³

In the predominantly Christian climate of nineteenth-century America, Yosemite also suggested an American Eden. The valley was protected on all sides by steep granite walls; it was lush and green, at least in spring, when the waterfalls were at their most spectacular; and its floor presented an open, park-like appearance because of the fires caused by lightning and the native peoples' controlled burning practices. Photographs from the nineteenth century confirm that Yosemite's floor had fewer trees and more open meadows than it has today.

California as a whole served equally well as an earthly Eden. In his first article about Yosemite, James Mason Hutchings described the Golden State in Edenic terms. 'There are', he wrote,

> but few lands that possess more of the beautiful and pic-
> turesque than California. Its towering and pine covered
> mountains; its widespread vallies [sic], carpeted with flowers;
> its leaping waterfalls; its foaming cataracts; its rushing rivers;
> its placid lakes; its evergreen forests; its gently rolling hills, with

Cathedral Spires and Cathedral Rocks, Yosemite,
and their reflections in a flooded meadow.

Light shining through trees, suggesting a 'great natural cathedral', 2006.

shrubs and trees and flowers, make this a garden of loveliness and a pride to her enterprising sons.[4]

Both Yosemite and California had their serpents – one literal, the other symbolic. At Yosemite the sight of an occasional rattlesnake only served to reinforce the Edenic parallel. The British traveller Lady Constance Gordon-Cumming remarked on the snakes she saw during her visit of 1878: 'We could not have such a Paradise without a serpent; and that it is a true garden of delight, is beyond question.'[5] The California Eden had its symbolic serpent: the Gold Rush era – a period of gross materialism – was considered analogous to the serpent, as it tempted men to leave homes and families in search of overnight success. The years following the Gold Rush were filled with racial prejudice, lynch law, mob rule and vigilance committees, evoking man's fall from grace and his expulsion from Eden. Despite these transgressions, Californians have continued to occupy their earthly paradise.

The area's native human inhabitants were more likely to dispel the visitor's image of Yosemite as Eden than to maintain it. The wooden shelters, mismatched clothing and subsistence lifestyle of the Miwok did much to erase lingering ideas about a race of noble savages in the

Sierra Nevada. Many nineteenth-century visitors would have agreed with Gordon-Cumming, who lamented that 'whatever dignity the American Indians may have possessed before they became familiar with their white brethren, those I have seen do not retain one vestige of the noble savage.'[6]

As a miniature Garden of Eden Yosemite seemed to confirm notions of Manifest Destiny – the belief held by white settlers that they had a God-given right to inhabit the entire continent. Where Yosemite evoked Eden, the state of California was considered a promised land. The travel writer Bayard Taylor called California 'a second Canaan for the impoverished and oppressed'.[7] Willard B. Farwell, a speaker addressing the Society of California Pioneers in 1859, called his audience the 'chosen people' and their arrival in California 'the fulfillment of the inscrutable and beneficent Divinity'.[8]

With the kindest of climates and the capacity to grow better and more abundant crops than any other locale in the country, California

Thomas Moran, 'A Vision of the Golden Country', engraving from Henry T. Williams, *The Pacific Tourist* (1876).

67

served equally well as the 'garden of the world'. Images like Thomas Moran's engraving *Vision of the Golden Country* reinforced this reputation in the mind of the public. In the foreground are the fruits and flowers grown by California farmers; in the background is Yosemite Valley, with its towering rock formations and rushing waterfalls; beyond Yosemite is the snowy crest of the Sierra Nevada mountain range. Even armchair travellers knew the 'flashing and golden pageant of California' and its 'sunny and ample lands', as described by the poet Walt Whitman.[9]

In the rush to print illustrated travel accounts about Yosemite, a few Eastern journals published wholly imaginary illustrations of the valley – images that may have been loosely based on early photographs, but which bore little resemblance to reality. This seems surprising given the many Yosemite photographs then in circulation. Perhaps in the early years of the valley's fame an imprecise rendering was considered better than no picture at all. *Ballou's Monthly Magazine* of Boston included fictitious Yosemite engravings on two occasions: the first in the issue of 21 May 1859, during the initial explosion of interest in the valley. That image, although inaccurate, seems loosely based on photographs of the waterfall.

Ballou's printed another problematic engraving in June 1870, during the publishing boom that followed completion of the transcontinental railroad. In it the three-tiered Yosemite Falls was drawn by *Ballou's* artist at one end of Yosemite Valley rather than in its actual location, midway along one side. A rock face reminiscent of El Capitan appears on the south side of the valley rather than on the correct north side. The text of the accompanying article was even less 'original' than the illustration, having been copied primarily from Samuel Bowles's travel book *Across the Continent*.

Of seven Yosemite lithographs published by the well-known American publishers Currier & Ives in the 1860s and early '70s, two differ significantly from photographs of the locale. One of these is *Yosemite Valley – California, 'The Bridal Veil' Fall*, drawn by Frances Flora Bond Palmer, an artist who often worked for the firm. Although its three rocky peaks are reminiscent of Yosemite, the rock pattern is wrong and the configuration of cascade, river and mountains seems fabricated. Another Currier & Ives print, *The Washington Columns*, also

terms of his 'flesh-and-bone tabernacle seem[ing] transparent as glass to the beauty about … as if truly an inseparable part of it, thrilling with the air and trees, streams and rocks, in the waves of the sun, – a part of all nature'.[22]

Muir was one of several liberal California thinkers who followed the call of nature and embraced it as a new form of spirituality. Such Nonconformists 'sought their religious experience and their source of personal stability outside all organizations, in nature itself'.[23] An incident in Muir's life gave him a powerful reason to equate one natural phenomenon, light, with the divine presence. After being blinded temporarily in an accident while operating machinery in 1867, Muir's vision was eventually restored; such an experience would have given added resonance to light's metaphorical power. In calling the Sierra Nevada mountains 'the Range of Light', Muir referred not only to the beauty and drama of this jagged, snowcapped range, but also to the numinous luminescence he believed emanated from it.

At Muir's invitation, Emerson made his own pilgrimage to Yosemite in the spring of 1871. The California naturalist invited the eastern sage to join him 'in a month's worship with nature in the high temples of the great Sierra Crown beyond our holy Yosemite'.[24] One of the most famous writers to visit the site, the noted Transcendentalist wrote very little about the experience, even in his journals. Riding with his companions, he commented, 'This Valley is the only place that comes up to the brag about it, and exceeds it.'[25] Despite his lack of literary exuberance, Emerson's companions noted that he enjoyed his stay a great deal. The Sage of Concord later wrote to his host regarding his happiness at finding Muir – 'the right man in the right place – in [his] mountain tabernacle'.[26]

Thirty-two years later, another famous visitor – President Theodore Roosevelt, popularly known as 'Teddy' – likewise sought out John Muir during his visit to Yosemite. The president and the naturalist spent three days together in 1903, camping and talking. Roosevelt later wrote that sleeping among the 'huge, cinnamon-colored trunks of the sequoias … was like lying in a great solemn cathedral, far vaster and more beautiful than any built by hand of man. Just at nightfall I heard, among other birds, thrushes which I think were Rocky Mountain hermits – the appropriate choir for such a place of worship.'[27]

Other Yosemite naturalists were equally spiritual, if more traditional in their religious beliefs than Muir. At times, both Clarence
King and Joseph LeConte imbued their scientific writings with religious
fervour. While a student at Yale, King praised science 'as almost a revelation'. He wrote to his friend James Gardner in 1861: 'I love science and
language dearly . . . [not] the practical minutiae . . . but the lofty laws of
creation[,] the connection of the material with the human[,] the esthetic
and the eternal, the cosmical relation of God's earthly planes.'[28]

LeConte, who began teaching geology and natural history at the
University of California at Oakland (later Berkeley) in 1869, brought
a similar background of traditional Christian beliefs to his exploration
of the Sierra Nevada. LeConte hoped to prove that science (specifically,
evolution) was 'entirely consistent with a rational theism and with other
fundamental religious beliefs'.[29] His ongoing interest in religion and
its relationship to science is amply illustrated by the titles of his books,
including *Evolution and its Relation to Religious Thought* and *The Religion
of a Man of Science*.

Diverging from the pattern of the first half of the century, much
of academic America was becoming increasingly convinced of the
necessity of separating religious and scientific writing. By 1860 the great
experiment of Protestant America – the attempt to unify knowledge and

President Teddy Roosevelt and John Muir at Glacier Point, Yosemite, with
Yosemite Falls in the distance, May 1903, gelatin silver stereograph.

belief – had failed in the east.[30] Like other scientists working at a distance from the mainstream of education and publishing, however, Muir, King and LeConte represented a pocket of resistance to this national trend.

Artists also found religious significance in the wonders of the Yosemite landscape. In 1863 the painter Albert Bierstadt and his writer friend Fitz Hugh Ludlow camped in the valley with friends. During his visit, Bierstadt referred to Yosemite as 'the Garden of Eden'.[31] Ludlow described the valley at greater length: 'I have lain awe-struck for six weeks between the two grandest leaves of the Almighty's album – those perpendicular white granite precipices which contain the wondrous Yo-Semite Valley.'[32] Having become something of a celebrity in New York City after publishing a novel titled *The Hasheesh Eater* in 1857, Ludlow wrote a series of articles about his western travels for the *New York Evening Post*.

Yosemite's unusual landscape may have brought Bierstadt and his friends to the valley, but its scenery appealed to them for symbolic as well as aesthetic reasons. In this they followed the precepts of the older Hudson River School artists who had perceived God in the landscapes of the eastern United States. The highly respected painter Asher B. Durand had urged young artists to study directly from nature. 'The external appearance of this our dwelling-place', he wrote in 1855, 'is fraught with lessons of high and holy meaning'.[33]

Bierstadt's beautiful small oil sketch *Valley of the Yosemite*, painted the year after their visit, conveys something of his spiritual response to the site. The glowing orange sunset evokes God's presence in the landscape, while the calm reflective water and the deer drinking at the water's edge suggest the peace and profound quiet of an Edenic locale. This small oil sketch would provide a template for several larger paintings over the next few years. The sky in these landscapes ranges from an Edenic pinkish-blue to a solemn dark purple and an apocalyptic bright orange.

For centuries light was used in church altarpieces to symbolize the divine presence. The light in American landscape paintings is symbolic but less overtly tied to biblical narratives; it comes from a source in nature, rather than an unseen spotlight located somewhere off-stage. Surprisingly only a few California painters emulated Bierstadt's use of light to convey a sense of spirituality. Yet the concept of a deity, whose very existence had been thrown into question by recent developments

Albert Bierstadt, *Valley of the Yosemite*, 1864, oil on paperboard.

in science, seemed then – and still seems today – immediately and happily obvious to many observers of the Yosemite landscape.

A painter could, to most viewers' satisfaction, demonstrate God's existence simply by delineating the most amazing of His creations. After the addition of convincing natural details to prove that the incredible valley was real, the inescapable conclusion was that the Great Creator alone could have sculpted such unique natural monuments. Most Yosemite paintings from the 1860s and '70s give evidence of the religious zeitgeist through a careful copying of the 'scripture of nature' Yosemite was purported to be. Intimate study of nature, as advocated earlier by Durand, was standard practice at Yosemite.

Modern viewers might ask whether careful delineation of empirical details actually conveys the spirituality intended by the artists. Natural details do not in themselves make this message clear to modern viewers; something else is usually required, like the glowing light in Bierstadt's landscapes, to complete the connection. It is only in hindsight, when considering the intricate interweaving of religion, science and art in the nineteenth century, that the importance of these specifics becomes clear. For those who believed as Emerson did that facts were the 'end or last issue of spirit' and that nature itself was 'the symbol of spirit', the minutiae of such an amazing landscape would have had evocative power even without the addition of glowing light or more blatant religious symbols.[34]

Although the early tourists had enjoyed worship services in the open air, the year-round residents of the valley soon felt the need for a more formal church building. Charles Geddes, a leading architect in San Francisco, was asked to construct a chapel in the valley. The resulting structure, built in 1879, still stands today: it is a New-England-style chapel with steep gables and board-and-batten walls. The Yosemite Chapel was erected by Mr E. Thomson, also of San Francisco, at a cost

The Yosemite Chapel, built 1879, with autumn foliage.

of \$3,000–\$4,000. According to James Mason Hutchings, the Yosemite Chapel was 'built by the California State Sunday School Association ... partly by subscriptions from the children, but mainly from the voluntary contributions of prominent members'.[35]

Hutchings noted that when the chapel bell rang its first notes on the evening of its dedication, it was the first 'church-going bell' ever heard in Yosemite. The Yosemite Chapel was originally built on high ground near the base of the Four Mile Trail to Glacier Point. In 1901 it was moved about a mile farther east, to another location near the south wall of the valley. Essentially it was moved from Lower Yosemite Village to the Upper Village after the latter had become the most heavily populated part of the valley. The Yosemite Chapel hosted its first wedding on 24 October 1884, when Harry L. Childs married Abbie Crippen, the eldest stepdaughter of hotel proprietor John Barnard.[36] The chapel was added to the National Register of Historic Places in 1973 – the first structure in the park to be so honoured.

Even today, images of Yosemite Valley maintain their power to evoke a spiritual response. To provide ambience during President-elect Barack Obama's inaugural luncheon in 2009, the United States Senate borrowed a Yosemite landscape by Thomas Hill to serve as backdrop

Inaugural luncheon for President Barack Obama with Thomas Hill's *Yosemite Valley*, borrowed for the event, 2009.

behind the president's table. The painting, which featured prominently in photographs of the event, seemed to convey a message of nationalistic pride in American scenery. During grace, however, when President Obama and the rest of the luncheon party bowed their heads in prayer, the painting's message became more religious, evoking thoughts of God's presence in nature. Despite the nineteenth-century shift from traditional Christian interpretations of Yosemite to more Transcendental responses, the valley's identification as a temple of nature, an American Eden and an earthly paradise has had great staying power.

FIVE

Artists' Mecca

Two years after Charles Weed took the first known photographs of Yosemite Valley (see chapter Two), another photographer, Carleton Watkins, launched an artistic competition when he travelled to the valley to take new views of the same subjects. During this visit in 1861, Watkins took the first 'mammoth plate' glass negatives used at Yosemite: sheets of glass approximately 46 × 56 cm (18 × 22 inches) in size. Because these glass-plate negatives were contact printed – placed directly on light-sensitive paper and then exposed to light – the size of the negatives determined the size of the prints.

Watkins' mammoth plate albumen prints were larger and more impressive than the 28 × 36-cm (11 × 14-inch) salt prints Weed made in 1859. When Weed returned to the valley for a second visit in 1863 or 1864, he accepted Watkins' challenge by bringing his own mammoth glass plate negatives.[1] When Watkins returned in 1866, the series he took (his second) included some of the most beautiful Yosemite photographs made by that date. Watkins sent six of these prints to the renowned journal *Philadelphia Photographer*, whose critic confirmed the general reaction to his Yosemite work: 'It has been said that "the pen is mightier than the sword," but who shall not say that in this instance, at least, the camera is mightier than the pen?'[2]

The British-born Eadweard Muybridge – christened Edward James Muggeridge – was the third photographer to document Yosemite extensively with his camera. Along with Watkins, he was one of the best. Muybridge probably visited the valley for the first time in May 1860,[3] but his first known Yosemite images were taken in 1867. This is the series he signed 'Helios', after the sun god of Greek mythology. One of these stereographs depicts his 'flying studio': his portable darkroom

Carleton Watkins, *Yosemite Falls (River View), 2,477 ft*,
1861, albumen photograph.

tent, bottles of photo-chemicals and boxes of glass negatives. Like
Weed and Watkins, Muybridge made much more impressive photographs during his second visit. Muybridge's mammoth plate views of
1872 were considered by many 'finer and more perfect than any which
have ever before been taken'.[4]

The travel writer Helen Hunt Jackson recommended Muybridge's
San Francisco studio as a fascinating addition to the tourist itinerary.
'I am not sure', she wrote, 'that there is anything so good to do in San
Francisco as to spend a forenoon in Mr. Muybridge's little upper
chamber, looking over these marvellous pictures.'[5] The competition
that began with Weed and Watkins ended in a draw between Watkins
and Muybridge, and both continue to have ardent proponents among
modern viewers.

The leading New York painter Albert Bierstadt came to the valley
in 1863, marking the advent of a more sophisticated era in Yosemite
landscape painting. Arriving in San Francisco, Bierstadt and his writer
friend Fitz Hugh Ludlow met up with two of Bierstadt's painter friends,

Eadweard Muybridge, *The Flying Studio (the Photographer's Chemicals and Equipment)*, 1867, albumen photograph.

Virgil Williams and Enoch Wood Perry; both were easterners who had moved to California in 1862. Their Yosemite party would also include John Hewston of San Francisco, described by Ludlow as a 'highly scientific metallurgist and physicist'.[6]

Although no diaries of their trip have come to light, Ludlow's published accounts provide many details of their adventure. During a stay that lasted about seven weeks, the painters began sketching in oils every day at dawn, while other members of the company spent their time 'sight-seeing, whipping the covert or the pool with various success for our next day's dinner, or hunting specimens of all kinds, – *Agassizing*, so to speak'.[7] The last is a reference to the eminent scientist Louis Agassiz.

Ludlow recorded their general movements in his book *The Heart of the Continent* (1870). Like many visitors, they entered Yosemite by the Mariposa Trail and stopped to admire the view from Inspiration Point. Reaching the valley floor, they set up their first camp in a meadow beside the Merced River, a mile or so west of Bridalveil Fall. They called this site 'Camp Rattlesnake' after an uninvited guest that crawled into Ludlow's blankets and was dispatched by Bierstadt. Their next campsite was five miles farther east, in a 'beautiful grove of oaks and cedars' opposite Yosemite Falls. Bierstadt and his friends moved on to the shore of Mirror Lake, deemed 'one of the loveliest places in the Valley' by Ludlow, and ended their stay in the vicinity of Vernal and Nevada Falls, behind Half Dome.

Bierstadt's Yosemite paintings captured the attention of the New York art world and the East Coast in general. After he returned to his New York studio, he began churning out canvas after canvas based on his Yosemite oil sketches. Like other members of the Hudson River School, his working method involved sketching landscapes and nature details in oil paint outdoors, *en plein air*, then turning those studies into

Eadweard Muybridge, *Valley of the Yosemite, from Rocky Ford*, 1872, albumen photograph.

larger, more complicated studio compositions. For the rest of the decade, buying a painting by Bierstadt was nearly synonymous with buying a Yosemite landscape.

Bierstadt's visit of 1863 did much to inspire local artists, both in their general commitment to landscape painting and their specific focus on Yosemite as subject. One writer noted that the effects of Bierstadt's stay were generally good, 'though they were first visible in a violent outbreak of Yosemite views, good, bad and indifferent'.[8] By 1868 California art critics were calling Yosemite 'the Mecca of all our artists'.

Foremost among the local painters to capture Yosemite on canvas were Thomas Hill and William Keith – 'our local stars', as a San Francisco socialite called them in her memoirs.[9] Keith painted an occasional Yosemite landscape along with many Sierra Nevada mountain scenes, but Hill assertively staked out the valley as his own artistic turf. Hill is the California artist most closely identified with enormous Yosemite panoramas painted for the captains of California industry, among them the railroad magnate Charles Crocker, his brother Judge Edwin Bryant Crocker, Governor Leland Stanford and the banker William C. Ralston.

The completion of the transcontinental railroad in 1869 gave East Coast and foreign artists easier access to Yosemite, and they arrived in ever-increasing numbers. Bierstadt returned to California from 1871 to 1873, spending part of his time in the High Sierra with the geologist Clarence King. While painting at Yosemite in 1872, he was photographed

William Keith, *Yosemite Valley*, 1875, oil on canvas.
Cathedral Rocks in the centre beyond the Merced River.

Thomas Hill, *Bridal Veil Falls, Yosemite*, 1895, oil on canvas. A later, very painterly canvas by Hill now in the White House in Washington, DC.

by Eadweard Muybridge, who also took pictures of glacial boulders and glacier-polished rock at the geologist's suggestion.[10]

Thomas Moran and William Bradford are among the illustrious eastern painters who visited during the 1870s, although their Yosemite canvases are not their most famous works. Moran is better known today for his Yellowstone and Grand Canyon subjects, and Bradford is noted for his paintings of icebergs. While in California, Bradford received quite a few commissions from wealthy Europeans on the Grand Tour. Baron Edmond James de Rothschild ordered five paintings of Arctic scenes in 1876; Victor Alexander Grosvenor, son of the Duke of Westminster, requested two Yosemite subjects in 1878. Other Yosemite canvases were acquired by Queen Victoria, Princess Louise, the Duke of Argyle, the Marquess of Dufferin and Baroness Burdett-Courts.[11] These landscapes may still exist in private collections.

A photograph made around 1869 gives modern viewers a sense of what it was like to paint in the mountains of California. Taken by Martin Mason Haseltine, it shows two painters working at Crescent Lake, located in the Sierra Nevada Mountains east of Wawona. The painter on the left appears to be the East Coast artist Gilbert Munger, making it likely that the painter on the right is John Ross Key, Munger's 'boon companion in his sketching tours'.[12]

Eadweard Muybridge, *Albert Bierstadt's Studio (Bierstadt Painting Native Encampment at Yosemite)*, 1872, albumen stereograph.

Martin Mason Hazeltine, *Crescent Lake, at Head of the Merced River (Artists Sketching), Mariposa Co.*, c. 1870, albumen stereograph.

Hazeltine's photograph illustrates many of the practices then current among landscape painters. Both artists have wooden boxes of oil paints that serve double duty as portable easels. These boxes contained slots in which wet canvas boards could be placed while the paint dried. Munger is seated on a folding campstool under a white parasol, used to keep direct sunlight off his canvas and himself. At the far right stands a man with a walking stick who was probably their hired guide. Hazeltine's photograph – like Muybridge's stereograph of Bierstadt painting a native encampment – shows that the photographers and painters working at Yosemite interacted socially and professionally.

Though in some ways typical of the wealthy travellers visiting Yosemite on the Grand Tour, Lady Constance Gordon-Cumming was unusual in documenting her stay in both pictorial and written form. Her display of Yosemite watercolours on the verandah of her hotel in 1878 was probably the first art exhibition held in the valley by a non-resident artist. To display her watercolours, she pinned them to sheets hung on the hotel porch.[13] Gordon-Cumming's travel account was published as a book, *Granite Crags*, in 1884.

Several photographers established seasonal studios in the valley, where they specialized in taking portraits of tourists with Yosemite Falls and other iconic sights in the background. The first was John James Reilly, who arrived in May 1870; after working in a cave opposite Yosemite Falls, he set up a canvas tent labelled 'J. J. Reilly's Stereoscopic View Manufactory'. Martin Mason Hazeltine – Reilly's primary competitor during the early 1870s – worked at Yosemite with a variety of partners during his five seasons in the valley.

By the 1880s Reilly and Hazeltine had been replaced by George Fiske and Gustavus Fagersteen as Yosemite's resident photographers.[14]

Eadweard Muybridge, *Ancient Glacier Channel, Lake Tenaya, Sierra Nevada Mountains*, 1872, albumen photograph.

During the winter of 1979–80, Fiske was the first photographer to live in the valley year-round.[15] The introduction of pre-sensitized dry-plate negatives made it possible to expose photographic plates any time – even in winter, when the wet-plate process was trickier than usual – and to develop them back in the studio, at leisure. Fiske's snow and storm images of the 1880s, made with dry plates, are much admired because they capture difficult weather conditions; through atmospheric effects, they convey mood or emotion.

Fiske made the valley his permanent residence after 1882. In addition to selling photographs at his studio, his work was available at the famous Big Tree Room of Barnard's Yosemite Falls Hotel (formerly Hutchings' Hotel). Fiske and his portable studio, nick-named the 'cloud-chasing chariot', were a familiar sight to Yosemite residents and visitors. His unpopulated landscape views were popular, as were humorous or sensational images such as *Dancing Girls at Glacier Point* (see p. 129), with its obvious appeal to tourists. Fiske lived at Yosemite until his death in 1918 and was buried in the valley's Pioneer Cemetery.

Women were also active in early Yosemite photography, although they usually played a supporting role as printers, retouchers and sales agents. The first to arrive may have been Sarah ('Sallie') Dutcher, who was working as a retoucher for Watkins in San Francisco by 1868 and came to the valley as his assistant in the 1870s. Later in the decade she operated a branch sales outlet for Watkins in San Francisco.[16]

John J. Reilly, *J. J. Reilly's Stereoscopic View Manufactory, Yosemite*, 1870s, albumen stereograph.

George Fiske and his 'Cloud-Chasing Chariot',
c. 1890, toned gelatin silver print.

Other unsung women in Yosemite's photographic industry included
'Pinkie' Ross, who sold George Fiske's and Isaiah Taber's photographs
at the Stoneman House Hotel, and Kate Crippen, who worked as a
printer for Fiske. Gertrude Towne, a niece of Fiske's wife, also assisted
in his studio. Kate Crippen's older sister Abigail worked as an agent

Thomas Hill's studio at Wawona, next to the Wawona Hotel, c. 1930s.

for both Fiske and Watkins, selling their work in the Big Tree Room.[17] Nellie Crockett Rivers, who came to Yosemite in 1889, initially worked as a waitress at the Stoneman House before she found employment developing, printing and retouching prints for Fiske. After her marriage to Charles Atkinson in 1892, Nellie and her husband turned their attention to forming an impressive collection of Native American baskets.[18]

A few painters also established studios in the valley to profit from the tourist trade. The first was Thomas Hill, who constructed his first Yosemite studio in 1883. Three years later he moved his base of operations to Wawona, where his daughter and her husband ran the Wawona Hotel; they built him a studio next to the hotel that became a tourist attraction in its own right. Charles D. Robinson, who began spending summers at Yosemite in 1880 and built a studio there in 1885, was Hill's resident competitor for many years. According to one source, Robinson sold at least 90 paintings to British tourists alone, including one acquired for the collection at Buckingham Palace.[19]

In 1899 the Norwegian-born Christian Jorgensen erected a studio near Sentinel Hotel that became, like Hill's, a tourist attraction. Travellers frequently dropped in to view his work; one of the most famous was President Teddy Roosevelt, who visited in 1903. As shown in photographs, Jorgensen's studio was decorated with framed artwork as well as 'skins, Indian rugs and curios . . . copper kettles . . . stuffed owls and eagles'.[20] Jorgensen and his wife formed a sizeable collection of Native American baskets, many of which they donated to the fledgling Yosemite Museum in the 1920s. In 1902 the California painter Harry Cassie Best established a Yosemite studio where he sold paintings and photographs for many years. After Best's death his daughter Virginia

Christian Jorgensen in his Yosemite studio, *c.* 1900.

R. Y. Young, *A Party of Camera 'Fiends' in Yosemite Valley*,
1902, half of a gelatin silver stereograph.

continued to operate the business with her husband, the photographer
Ansel Adams.

After Kodak introduced its famous camera and roll film in 1888,
cameras became easier to operate and photography was no longer the
domain of the professional. Amateur photography soared in popularity
by the mid-1890s, and many of the first photography clubs were formed
that decade. Groups such as the California Camera Club (founded in
1890) arranged photographic field trips for their members. R. Y.
Young's stereograph *A Party of Camera 'Fiends' in Yosemite Valley* gives
evidence that such groups visited Yosemite to capture its spectacular
scenery. A local amateur was Celia Crocker, whose father founded

Crocker's Sierra Resort on the western edge of Yosemite Valley in 1880. Crocker documented the valley between 1889 and 1903.[21]

ARTISTS, SOME OF THEM QUITE FAMOUS, continued to visit Yosemite in the twentieth century, although the valley was no longer the artists' Mecca it had been in the 1860s and '70s. Discarding the detailed, quasi-scientific Hudson River mode of nineteenth-century painters, the artists of the new century adopted newer styles and a more subjective, interpretive approach to art. A few photographers captured Yosemite subjects in the soft-focus, intimate manner of Pictorialism and Tonalism. Artist-photographers including Anne Brigman, Alvin Langdon Coburn and William E. Dassonville created moody, sombre images that expressed their personal response to nature.

In the second decade of the twentieth century, the California Impressionists Colin Campbell Cooper and Maurice Braun painted a few Yosemite landscapes, although most of their painter colleagues considered the valley passé. Like the Pictorialists, Cooper and Braun worked in what they considered a more up-to-date style. Impressionism, with

Anne Brigman, *The Lone Pine*, 1908, vintage gelatin silver print.

Colin Campbell Cooper, *Half Dome, Yosemite*, oil on canvas.

its beautiful bright colours and loose brushwork, was more interpretive and less detail-driven than earlier painting styles.

The tourist market at the turn of the century supported a growing number of commercial photographers, including Daniel J. Foley, Julius Boysen and Henry G. Peabody. They were followed in turn by Arthur C. Pillsbury and Ralph Anderson. The last worked for the National Park Service from 1932 to 1953. Their Yosemite images were used in promotional literature and other publications about the park during the first half of the twentieth century.[22]

Yosemite's commercial photographers often complained about the competition they faced when taking souvenir portraits at the most popular tourist locations. A letter written in 1916 to Julius Boysen brings this into sharp focus. Park Superintendent W. B. Lewis wrote to Boysen,

Due to the annoyance to which the public would be subjected by the presence of three photographers at these places at the same time, each jockeying for position and soliciting for permission to photograph groups, I am not in favor of permitting competitive service. I see no reason why the three parties interested, yourself, Mr Best, and Mr Pillsbury, cannot get together in an arrangement . . . by which each has the sole privilege every third day for doing group work at Mirror Lake and Happy Isles.[23]

Arthur Pillsbury's career is particularly interesting. Pillsbury operated a studio in Yosemite Valley from 1907 until 1928, when the building was destroyed by fire. He made headlines in 1910 when he photographed San Francisco and Los Angeles from a hot air balloon and wrote his own account of flying above LA for *Sunset* magazine.[24] In 1916 Pillsbury was featured in the press again when he drove his new Studebaker Six car to the edge of Overhanging Rock at Glacier Point.

Ansel Adams, the most famous of all Yosemite photographers, first visited the park in 1916 during a family vacation. Already interested in nature, Adams developed a parallel passion for photography after his father gave him a Kodak Brownie Box camera for the trip.[25] The following year he joined the Sierra Club and returned to Yosemite with better photographic equipment. Adams's dramatic black-and-white photographs proved him as a worthy heir of Watkins and Muybridge. Adams's name is virtually synonymous today with the most sublime aspects of Yosemite scenery, although some critics have found his exclusion of human beings and man-made constructions ironic, given the valley's increasing congestion in the twentieth century. Less famous are the commercial images Adams took for the national park and its concessionaires – images that were used in brochures and other publications about the park.

The notable modernist painters William and Marguerite Zorach camped at Yosemite in 1920 to paint its scenery. During their stay, William went mountain climbing with Ansel Adams, who was then eighteen. The painter noted proudly that he 'walked 40 miles with a 60 pound pack of sketching material to the big sequoias so as to get the feeling of the country as those men who first got there'.[26] Like Bierstadt half a century earlier, the Zorachs considered Yosemite 'the Garden of Eden' and 'God's paradise'. Although William Zorach had trouble sleeping out of doors, by his own account he 'sketched and painted in ecstasy'.[27]

Arthur C. Pillsbury's Studebaker Six on overhanging rock, Glacier Point, 1916.

The Japanese-born painter Chiura Obata had a very different response to the park seven years later. 'Yosemite Valley', he noted, 'is crowded with automobiles and the road is shiny with oil'. Obata disliked the look of camping in the valley: 'The tents, and occasionally a cabin, stand in between pine and cypress trees according to their numbers . . . It has the appearance of camping in a tent as someone advertised, but compared to camping in the mountains it looks like living in a can.' Obata noted that most campers ate at restaurants and cafeterias, and the road near the general store was 'crowded with cars: bumper to bumper like a school of sardines'.[28]

Unlike their nineteenth-century predecessors, the Zorachs and Obata ignored the details of nature in favour of a more streamlined, modernist depiction of the landscape. Their response to nature was more subjective and expressive, less scientific. The Zorachs' colourful, simplified images were influenced by the European art movements Cubism and Fauvism. Obata's work, with its calligraphic outlines and simple shapes, owes much to his Japanese heritage.

The famous modernist painter Georgia O'Keeffe joined Ansel Adams for a seventeen-day horseback excursion in September 1938, along with David McAlpin of New York's Museum of Modern Art. O'Keeffe painted very few Yosemite landscapes as a result of this trip, but her presence prompted Adams to take new photographs of the valley. 'To see O'Keeffe in Yosemite is a revelation', Adams wrote to her husband, the photographer Alfred Stieglitz. 'Her mood and the mood of the place [are] not a conflict, but a strange, new mixture for me. She actually stirred me up to photograph Yosemite all over again.'[29]

The photographer Edward Weston, another friend of Adams, came to Yosemite in 1937 and 1938. Weston travelled with the support of a Guggenheim Fellowship – the first ever awarded to a photographer – which freed him to take photographs throughout the west and southwest, despite the Great Depression then in progress. At Yosemite he was particularly inspired by the twisted juniper trees at Lake Tenaya, although he also photographed scenery on the valley floor, including Ansel Adams's darkroom building.

overleaf: William Zorach, *Half Dome, Yosemite*, 1920,
watercolour and pencil on paper.

William Zorach 1950.

Chiura Obata, *El Capitan*, 1931, colour woodblock print.

Ansel Adams, *Clearing Winter Storm, Yosemite National Park, California*, 1944, gelatin silver print.

Although Adams is famous for his photographs, he was also active as an environmentalist. His first photographs and writings were published in the Sierra Club *Bulletin*, and in 1934 he was elected a member of the Sierra Club Board of Directors, a post he would hold for 37 years. During his tenure the Sierra Club evolved into a powerful national organization devoted to the creation of national parks and protection of the natural environment.

Adams's artistic reputation skyrocketed in the 1970s. In September 1979 *Time* magazine declared him 'the most popular "fine" photographer in America'.[30] A mural-size print of his famous *Clearing Winter Storm, Yosemite National Park* made headlines in 2010 when it sold for $772,500.[31] At the time of writing, that is still the highest price ever paid for a Yosemite photograph (although photographs of other subjects have sold for millions of dollars).

In recognition of his work as both photographer and conservationist, Adams received the Conservation Service Award, the Interior Department's highest civilian honour, in 1968. In 1980 he was awarded

Charles Cramer, *Snow-covered Trees, El Capitan*, 1997,
digital colour photograph.

the Presidential Medal of Freedom for his efforts to 'preserve this
country's wild and scenic areas, both on film and on earth'.[32] Six months
after Adams's death in 1984, Congress passed legislation designating
more than 200,000 acres southeast of Yosemite the Ansel Adams
Wilderness Area. Like Carleton Watkins a century earlier, Adams was
also honoured by having a California mountain named for him:
Mount Ansel Adams is a 3,584-metre (11,760-foot) peak on the
southeast boundary of the park.

The Ansel Adams Gallery at Yosemite is now in its third generation of family ownership. In 1971 Ansel and Virginia Adams turned over the business to their son Michael and his wife Jeanne, who continue to sell photographs by a wide variety of artists. Adams and his followers have inspired a proliferation of scenic imagery in what might be called the 'Sierra Club style'. Whether they work in black-and-white or colour, these photographers focus on the beauties of nature – both in close-up details and scenic vistas – rather than the inhabited portions of the valley. Some practitioners of this style, like Charles Cramer and John Sexton, studied with Adams himself. Others – Robert Glenn Ketchum, David Muench and the late Galen Rowell – did not study with Adams, but work in a similar vein. Although considered old-fashioned by the art world, which places a premium on novelty and innovation, their photographs are loved by millions of viewers worldwide.

In the twentieth century tourists and amateur photographers far outnumbered other groups of Yosemite image-makers, and the snap-shots they produced – both black-and-white and colour – have become ubiquitous. As photographers adjusted to new media at the turn of the century, photos printed from film were rapidly outnumbered by their digital descendants. Charles Cramer, a one-time student of Ansel Adams, commented that 'There was a steep learning curve, with scanning and Photoshop, but it soon became clear that digital allowed ultimate control over the final print – I'm convinced Ansel would be pleased!'[33] Cramer is proud that in 1997 his image *Snow-covered Trees, El Capitan* was the first digital print sold by the Ansel Adams Gallery. Cramer's success is one indication among many that Yosemite continues to inspire amateur and professional artists alike, even as photographers respond to the digital revolution.

SIX

The Park Idea

As the first American wilderness area preserved primarily for its scenic values, Yosemite holds a special place in the history of the country's national parks. The valley itself was made a California State Park in 1864 by a special Act of Congress, but historians have argued convincingly that Yosemite was the first national park de facto, if not de jure (in fact, if not by law).[1] Not only was the valley designated a park in 1864 by federal legislation, but its protected status was upheld against potentially conflicting state law in 1868 when the United States Senate refused to ratify California legislation allowing private claims in the valley.

The Yosemite grant led the way for later acts of legislation establishing parks at Yellowstone, Niagara and other scenic locations. Yellowstone, land of hot springs and geysers, was declared the first official national park in 1872. Unlike Yosemite, which was located in a state with an established government that could oversee park management, Yellowstone was located in the Wyoming Territory, with no local government to take control; placing it under federal management seemed the logical course of action. Niagara Falls and its surroundings, already endangered by rampant commercial development, were belatedly declared a state park and nature reserve in 1885.

Fundamental to any study of Yosemite is the valley's role in the expansion of the park idea beyond urban islands of pastoral preservation to encompass wilderness areas threatened by human encroachment. One of the first urban parks was Boston Common, a central green established in Massachusetts in 1634. Although the common is an ancient concept, Boston Common is often considered the first urban American park; by 1830 it was used solely for recreational purposes, rather than for grazing sheep and other utilitarian activities. Mount Auburn Cemetery near Boston, created in 1831, was the first 'garden' or 'rural'-style cemetery in the United States, and is credited with launching the American public parks and gardens movement.[2] Designed with winding paths, scenic vistas, groves of trees and several small lakes and ponds, Mount Auburn was a far cry from earlier cemeteries, with their regular rows of gravestones located in close proximity to churches.

In England the 1840s saw the creation of Princes Park near Liverpool and Birkenhead Park in Birkenhead, both designed by Joseph Paxton; Birkenhead has been called the first publicly funded urban park in the world.[3] The American landscape architect Frederick Law Olmsted visited Birkenhead Park in 1850, and Paxton's influence is clear in the appearance of New York's Central Park, designed by Olmsted and his partner Calvert Vaux in 1857. A few years later Olmsted was working in California, where Yosemite's open fields, groves of trees and winding river clearly suggested a natural park.

From the beginning, Yosemite presented an awkward dichotomy between settled tourist areas (the valley itself) and remote mountain scenery (the surrounding Sierra Nevada mountains). California in general and Yosemite in particular were never considered 'wilderness' in quite the same way as other parts of the American West. Because of its coastal location, California was settled earlier than the interior of the continent. The journey to Yosemite was difficult even after coach roads were constructed in the 1870s, but it was never as arduous as the early expeditions across the Great Plains, up the Missouri River or across the Rockies. In fact, only four years after the valley was first seen by the Mariposa Battalion, early civilian visitors were already calling themselves 'tourists'.

Accounts of the rigours of the trip varied from author to author, but most found it tiring rather than dangerous. The famous publisher Horace Greeley, who made the excursion in record time in 1859, found it merely a 'weary, interminable ride'.[4] Another tourist that year felt all his fears vanish upon learning that the party ahead of them contained three young ladies – 'Col. Frémont's daughter and niece with their cousin'.[5] After several visits to Yosemite between 1870 and 1875, Brantz Mayer, an employee of the u.s. Army, noted that Yosemite coach drivers and tour guides exaggerated the difficulty of the trip to make female

El Capitan Meadow, looking edenic and park-like in sunlight.

tourists more careful and 'to make them believe they are doing something very great'. Mayer nevertheless warned his wife, who had been ill, that visitors needed to be in 'tip-top condition' to make the journey.[6]

Israel Ward Raymond, California representative of the Central American Steamship Transit Company of New York, may have been the first to consider preserving Yosemite as a park. Although J. W. Edmonds, commissioner of the General Land Office, penned the Yosemite legislation, it was Raymond who asked that his own senator, John Conness of California, introduce the bill before Congress.[7] To underscore the validity of the request, Raymond sent Conness some of Carleton Watkins's photographs of the valley as proof of its spectacular appearance. The landscape architect Frederick Law Olmsted was long thought to have drafted the park proposal, but his biographers have found no evidence he did so.[8] In fact, his first documented visit to Yosemite occurred in August 1864, six weeks after the Yosemite bill was signed by President Abraham Lincoln.

Raymond and Edmonds had support from many impressive colleagues: Thomas Starr King, the prominent Unitarian minister who had published a book on the glories of nature back east; Judge Stephen Field, who saw the need for a state geological survey; and John F. Morse, a leading California physician. Josiah D. Whitney, the State Geologist, was a strong lobbyist for the park, as was Jessie Benton Frémont, wife of the well-known explorer Colonel John C. Frémont and daughter of the western expansionist Senator Thomas Hart Benton of Missouri.[9] The Frémonts were familiar with Yosemite, having owned the nearby Mariposa Estate and Mining Company from 1847 to 1859.

Senator Conness introduced the bill on 17 May 1864, and President Lincoln signed it on 30 June, establishing the Yosemite Grant. The following month, Governor Frederick F. Low signed a state bill provisionally accepting Yosemite's protected status on behalf of California. Official acceptance of the park occurred on 2 April 1866, during the next session of the California state legislature.

The idyllic appearance of the valley floor may have contributed to the rapidity with which Yosemite was preserved for the public; designating the valley a park seemed logical because it already resembled one. Yosemite had flat grassy meadows, scattered clusters of trees, a winding river with occasional sandy beaches, and orchards and gardens planted by early residents. The travel writer John Todd commented on the 'lawns, smooth as a garden' that he saw while riding through the valley.[10] The geologist Clarence King described Yosemite as a 'smooth river-cut park' with 'exquisite perfection of finish'.[11]

In the nineteenth century the valley floor had fewer trees and more open fields than it has today because of fires – natural or set by the Native Americans who lived there – that periodically cleared out small trees and undergrowth. This is clear in early Yosemite photographs and paintings. With the gradual increase in Anglo-Americans living in the valley Yosemite became increasingly forested, a fact noticed by visitors as early as the 1880s.

Yosemite's development as a park is interwoven with the history of the painters and photographers who publicized its scenic wonders. Watkins's Yosemite photographs played a significant historical role when Congress was deliberating whether to set aside the valley as a park. Legend has it that they were even sent to the White House, where President Lincoln studied them prior to signing the Yosemite bill. Whether or not this is true, Watkins's prints were later displayed in the office of the Sergeant at Arms of the United States Senate, and must have been widely known among legislators in the nation's capital.[12]

Bierstadt's early Yosemite paintings are also thought to have played a role in convincing legislators to approve designation of the park.

Carleton Watkins's Yosemite photographs on display in the office of the
Sergeant at Arms of the United States Senate, 1869–79.

Although his first public exhibition of a Yosemite canvas did not occur
until April 1864, Yosemite landscapes were previously on display in the
painter's New York studio where they were seen by the business and
social leaders who fraternized with the well-connected artist.[13] Knowledge of Yosemite had been spreading for several years, but Bierstadt's
paintings provided eastern viewers with their first living-colour visions
of its sublime scenery.

After Yosemite was designated a state park in 1864, California
governor Frederick F. Low appointed a Board of Commissioners to
oversee park management. The original Board included Governor
Low himself; Josiah D. Whitney, State Geologist; William Ashburner,
a mining engineer and member of Whitney's geological survey team;
Israel Ward Raymond of the Central American Steamship Transit

Company; E. S. Holden, a businessman from Stockton, California; Alexander Deering, an attorney from Mariposa; George W. Coulter, a Coulterville merchant; Galen Clark, an innkeeper from Wawona; and the landscape architect Frederick Law Olmsted, who was then managing the Mariposa Estate.[14] Olmsted was elected chairman and by-laws were written calling for two meetings a year, one in the valley and one in San Francisco.

Already an expert on park and landscape issues, Olmsted was an early proponent of park preservation in the developing battle between preservation and development forces. He drafted a management plan on 9 August 1865 that would later be hailed as a classic statement of the ideals of park management. 'The first point to be kept in mind', he wrote, 'is the preservation and maintenance as exactly as is possible of the natural scenery.'[15]

Although Olmsted proposed a series of roads, trails and bridges for Yosemite, his designs were sympathetic to the natural environment and would have allowed tourists to experience the park in relative comfort without allowing excessive development to affect the scenery. Olmsted even wrote to the painters Thomas Hill and Virgil Williams and the photographer Carleton Watkins, who were then camping at Yosemite, to ask their opinions on aesthetic aspects of managing the valley – probably the first time American artists were consulted officially on such a topic.[16]

Olmsted's plan might have been more influential had the Yosemite Commissioners not included two men who opposed it: Josiah D. Whitney and William Ashburner. When Olmsted requested $37,000 in state funding to implement improvements to the park, Whitney and Ashburner feared the request would divert funds away from the Geological Survey. They blocked his park management plan from reaching the state legislature, and it fell into obscurity until it was published by Olmsted's biographer nearly a century later.[17]

After Olmsted returned to New York the following year, there was no one on site to monitor commercial development in the valley. From the beginning, a pattern was thus established in which commercial interests gained support to the detriment of scenic preservation. Although Olmsted's tenure at Yosemite was brief, it was memorialized when Olmsted Point near Tenaya Lake was later named in his honour.

Galen Clark, one of the original Commissioners, was appointed the park's first Guardian in 1866. Clark is one of the most interesting personalities in Yosemite history.[18] He arrived in California around the time of the Gold Rush, but developed a lung infection that was diagnosed as 'consumption' (tuberculosis). After Clark's doctor urged him to seek rest and outdoor air, he moved to Wawona, southwest of Yosemite Valley, near the Mariposa Grove of Big Trees. Clark may not have been the first white American to see the Mariposa Grove, but he was probably the first to count and measure its trees.

In 1857 Clark established a rustic inn, called Clark's Station, on the Wawona route to Yosemite. There he acted as host and guide to travellers passing through, furnishing them with shelter, meals, a place to graze their horses and tours of the Mariposa Grove. While staying at his inn, visitors were entertained with information on Yosemite plants and animals, geology and native life. Clark served as Guardian of the park for much of the nineteenth century: from 1866 to 1880, and again from 1889 to 1897. Living to the venerable age of 95, he became a resident expert on the area.

Carleton Watkins, *Galen Clark at the Mariposa Grove of Big Trees*, 1861, half of an albumen stereograph.

Charles Bierstadt, *Clark's Hotel, Mariposa, California*, 1872–3,
half of an albumen stereograph.

John Muir, who arrived on the scene in 1868, would have approved
of Olmsted's vision for the park. From the beginning Muir was concerned with what we now call ecological issues. Climbing to the summit
of Mount Wilson in California's San Gabriel Mountains in 1875, he
was appalled by the destruction caused by sheep, which he called 'hoofed
locusts'.[19] By the late 1880s Muir had turned his attention to the floor
of Yosemite Valley, where there had been a dramatic increase in hotels,
shops and support services.

Muir felt that state management of the valley had been a disaster,
and he began to lobby for a new cause: the establishment of a national
park at Yosemite. Muir asked his photographer friend George Fiske

to take pictures of some of the activities he considered detrimental to the park: a section of valley floor ploughed over for hay, hundreds of tree stumps left by the creation of 'state pasturage' and uncontrolled trimming of trees. Fiske's photographs of 1890 are important as early propaganda images made in the service of an environmental cause.

Engravings based on Fiske's photographs were used as illustrations for an article Muir published in *The Century Magazine* in 1890, during his crusade to establish a national park. The article was titled 'The Treasures of the Yosemite' and it was followed by a sequel the next month, 'Features of the Proposed Yosemite National Park'.[20] Muir's articles contained engravings based on work by a number of artists. Except for Fiske's photographs, the rhetorical bias of the illustrations was positive, presenting the valley's features to their best advantage and making a case for national park status based on the spectacular scenery of the valley.

Muir had considerable support in his crusade to pry Yosemite away from state management. Three friends published letters in *The Century Magazine* in January 1890, focusing attention on improper management of the state park and the surrounding area. The writers were George G. Mackenzie, author of a recent Yosemite guidebook; Lucius P. Deming, a judge in Connecticut; and Robert Underwood Johnson, editor of *The Century Magazine*. The last had accompanied Muir on a two-week trip to Yosemite Valley and Tuolumne Meadows the previous summer to see their condition in person. Mackenzie revived Olmsted's idea of soliciting professional advice on aesthetic aspects of park management. He recommended that the Yosemite Commission include an eminent landscape gardener, since under the current management, 'artistic instinct ... has been sacrificed to the commercial'. Deming likewise called for 'a cultivated taste' in park management and Johnson urged that Yosemite Valley be placed 'in the hands of the very best experts'.[21]

A few months later, an article titled 'Amateur Management of the Yosemite Scenery' appeared in *The Century Magazine* by an unidentified writer (perhaps the journal's editor, Robert Underwood Johnson). The author lamented the fact that Olmsted's management advice had been ignored. Had Olmsted's suggestions been followed, he noted, Yosemite visitors would not have witnessed 'the spectacle of the most phenomenal of the national pleasure grounds ignorantly hewed and hacked, sordidly plowed and fenced, and otherwise treated on principles of forestry which would disgrace a picnic ground'.[22]

The Southern Pacific Railroad was an ally in the national park crusade, with Muir calling on friends in railroad management to support the cause. As he said rather tactlessly to the Sierra Club years later, 'Even the soulless Southern Pacific R. R. Co., never counted on for anything good, helped nobly in pushing the bill for this park through Congress.'[23] Railroad management was, of course, working in their own best interest: they helped to safeguard a scenic attraction that would draw additional tourists, many of whom would arrive by rail.

The efforts of Muir and his allies were ultimately successful: in October 1890 some 3,885 square kilometres (1,500 square miles) surrounding the valley were placed under federal protection and designated Yosemite National Park. Muir's wish that the valley itself be transferred to federal management would not be fulfilled until early the following century. Thus from 1890 to 1906, Yosemite Valley was administered as a small state park in the centre of a large national park.

Two years after helping to establish Yosemite National Park, Muir's efforts to found a 'Yosemite Defense Association' resulted in the creation of the Sierra Club. Meeting in San Francisco in May 1892, Muir founded the club with a lawyer named Warren Olney and a group of professors from Stanford University and the University of California at Berkeley. They based the structure of the club on that of the Appalachian Mountain Club, formed sixteen years earlier in the east. Muir was elected as the first president and served in that role until his death in 1914.

As a state park, Yosemite had been managed by a Guardian and a Board of Commissioners. In 1891 the u.s. Army was brought in to manage the national park. Among the troops were the so-called 'Buffalo Soldiers', African American troops who were among the country's first park rangers. (Their nickname was bestowed by the Cheyenne and other Plains Indians, who considered their dark curly hair similar to the matted fur on the heads of buffalo.) Muir and his friends had been unhappy with state oversight of the park and felt the Army would be an improvement. Their complaints convinced John Noble, then Secretary of the Interior, to go straight to President Benjamin Harrison with their request. The Army was given management of Yosemite and two other

U.S. Army, Sixth Cavalry, Troop F, posing with 'Fallen Monarch'
sequoia tree, Mariposa Grove, 1899.

national parks in California – Sequoia and General Grant – all of them
established in the autumn of 1890.[24] Muir was especially pleased
because mounted troops would have considerable clout when stopping
sheep owners from grazing their herds inside park borders.

The Army provided exactly the muscle and conviction Muir wanted.
In 1895 private landowners living within the boundaries of the park
were charged with a number of park violations. California governor
James H. Budd wrote to the Army, requesting leniency in their treatment.
Captain Alex Rodgers, commander of the Army unit charged with protecting Yosemite, replied with 'a detailed account of infractions by local
landowners that would "entirely defeat the purpose of the law establishing the park".'[25] On another occasion, the Army's Lieutenant Colonel
S.B.M. Young forcibly expelled six prominent Bay Area industrialists
and a lawyer who were hunting illegally in Yosemite's backcountry.
Young met the complaints lodged by these high-profile malefactors
with logic and determination, gaining the support of local citizens and
winning the day. The Army would have jurisdiction until 1914, when
civilian rangers were put in charge. The National Park Service took
over when it was founded in 1916.

In the early twentieth century Muir renewed his campaign to have
Yosemite Valley and the Mariposa Grove of Big Trees placed under

federal control. President Teddy Roosevelt, who visited Yosemite in 1903, became an important ally in this cause. Roosevelt visited Yosemite during a trip through the west that also included Yellowstone and the Grand Canyon. The president left San Francisco for Yosemite on 15 May 1903, accompanied by Muir, California governor George Pardee, and Benjamin Ide Wheeler, president of the University of California.

After visiting the Mariposa Grove of Big Trees – which Roosevelt loved – Muir and the president spent three days camping together at Yosemite. Roosevelt proclaimed Muir 'the companion above all others for such a trip'. Muir was then 65 years old – twenty years older than the president – and an important leader among California preservationists. The two men left the larger party behind, accompanied on their camping trip by only 'two packers and three pack mules'.[26] They slept under the stars and talked at length over the campfire; Muir even entertained the president one night by dancing a jig.[27] During their travels, the two men posed for photographs in the Big Tree Grove and atop Glacier Point Cliff. The latter image has become an icon of American national parks, the Sierra Club and the environmental movement.

During their excursion Muir did everything he could to convince President Roosevelt of the need to place Yosemite Valley under federal

President Teddy Roosevelt, John Muir and travelling party with the 'Grizzly Giant' (Roosevelt and Muir in centre), Mariposa Grove, Yosemite, 1903.

protection. State control of the valley, he argued, was allowing adverse development. Muir also called on railroad magnate Edward H. Harriman, whose empire included the Southern Pacific, Union Pacific and Illinois Central lines.[28] Harriman helped convince the California legislature to approve the state's transfer bill in 1905, and a year later he helped send the bill to Congress: President Roosevelt signed HJ Res. 118 on 11 June 1906, adding Yosemite Valley and the Mariposa Grove of Big Trees to Yosemite National Park.

In 1908 President Roosevelt honoured John Muir's efforts by naming a grove of redwood trees north of San Francisco the 'Muir Woods National Monument'. Since that time, many natural areas, landscape features, institutions and animals have been named in honour of the California naturalist. These include Muir Beach near San Francisco, Mount Muir in the Sierra Nevada Mountains, Muir Glacier in Alaska and the John Muir Trail, which climbs from the floor of Yosemite Valley to the top of Mount Whitney (named after the geologist Josiah D. Whitney). In addition to a college named for Muir in southern California, there are buildings named for him at the University of Edinburgh and Heriot-Watt University, also in Edinburgh, Scotland. Muir's name also appears in the scientific nomenclature of a mineral, two species of aster, a member of the rose family, a type of wren, a subspecies of alpine rabbit, a millipede and a butterfly.[29]

In the nineteenth century Olmsted, Muir and others wrote of wilderness as a source of health and well-being. Nowadays, beyond providing a setting for camping, hiking and other outdoor activities, wilderness is still credited with the power to comfort and heal. Following the terrorist attacks of 11 September 2001, then-Secretary of the Interior Gale Norton announced that entrance fees to the national parks would be waived over Veterans Day weekend in early November 'to allow Americans the opportunity to seek solace and inspiration from the Nation's parks, monuments, and memorials'. Norton commented, 'What better places to begin that healing process than in our parks, where Americans can draw strength from national icons of freedom and peace, from splendors of nature . . . and reconnect with the values that have made this nation great.'[30]

SEVEN

Tourists, Tolls and Trains

In 1875 John Muir complained about the growth in Yosemite tourism, using analogies befitting a naturalist: 'As soon as the winter snow melts,' he wrote, 'an ungovernable avalanche of tourists comes pouring pell mell into Yosemite, flooding the hotels, and chafing and grinding against one another like rough-angled bowlders [sic] in a pothole.'[1] Like serious backpackers today, Muir was happy to escape to the mountains, leaving the valley floor to the tourists. The geologist Clarence King complained more specifically about the 'army of literary travelers' who had visited Yosemite, noting that they all felt compelled to describe the view from Inspiration Point. 'Here,' he wrote, 'all who make California books, down to the last and most sentimental specimen who so much as meditates a letter to his or her local paper, dismount and inflate.'[2]

King's 'army of literary travellers' had been immensely successful at promoting Yosemite tourism. They included Josiah D. Whitney (who published the first Yosemite guidebook), and the journalist Horace Greeley (known today for the phrase 'Go West, young man, go West!'). These and other writers published guidebooks and articles describing their travels, and their advice provided later tourists with suggestions on topics ranging from the best routes to the valley, the cost of hotels and guides, and the importance of wearing a dustcoat or 'duster' to protect one's clothing during the stagecoach ride across the dry central valley of California.

While the duster was recommended for travellers of both genders, the 'bloomer' costume was considered a necessity for female visitors. Bloomers were loose trousers gathered at the ankles or below the knee and worn under a short skirt. They were required for horseback riding

'The Bloomer Polka', *c.* 1850s, detail of sheet music cover.
Bloomers were considered the most appropriate clothing
for women riding horseback into Yosemite Valley.

in the mountainous areas around the valley, where riding side-saddle
was too dangerous. A 'lady correspondent' for the *Sacramento Union*
wrote in 1868 that 'All of our most refined and fastidious ladies who
have enjoyed that never-to-be-forgotten trip went prepared with
bloomers, or were glad to use scissors and needle in improvising such
a suit before getting to the valley.'[3]

Despite the freedom of movement bloomers allowed, many women were relieved when it came time to don normal attire again. One young lady wrote that before leaving in Hutchings's stagecoach, the women in her party 'got ready (by putting on our bloomers)'. After riding to Gentry's Station, where they would spend the night, she and her friends were 'perfectly wild for pleasure to be able to change our clothes'.[4]

Guidebook writers addressed a wide variety of topics, from the practical to the aesthetic. Their descriptions of Yosemite scenery resonate with faint echoes of John Ruskin's writings on the aesthetic values of mountains and water, and Edmund Burke's treatise on the Sublime and the beautiful. The writer of the Yosemite edition of the *Nelson's Pictorial Guide-books* series, for example, declared that Yosemite Falls produced more turbulent emotions than did picturesque spots like Mirror Lake: 'You confront the great falls almost with a sense of apprehension and a feeling of undefinable awe: but you look upon this crystal mirror with a sentiment of subdued admiration.'[5]

As early as 1859 there was, surprisingly, a toll of $1 per person on the Merced River ferry. By the late 1870s, there were tolls on the trails into the valley ($1 per person); entry and exit fees (50 cents); and tolls on the trails to Glacier Point and Nevada Falls (also $1). With horses and guides priced at $2.50 or $3 a day, strangers often grouped together to share the guide's fee.

In the late 1860s hotels in Yosemite Valley cost $3.50 a day. Since the price of San Francisco hotels averaged $2 to $2.50 a day ($3 for the more elegant Cosmopolitan, Grand and Occidental), hotels in the valley were hardly a bargain. Their tariffs were even less justifiable considering the rustic accommodations available. Nowadays there is only one fee to enter the park, and the tolls on trails have long been eliminated. There are, nevertheless, extra charges for hotels, campsites and special activities like horseback riding.

Travellers in the early 1870s estimated the total cost of the trip at about $100. One visitor, Brantz Mayer, tallied his expenses at $108.60 for eleven days, concluding that 'a little less than $10 *per diem*' was 'pretty moderate for such a journey'. Although he found the cost moderate, Mayer lamented that 'the people who haunt the valley, keep the taverns, hire the horses, act as *guides*', and so forth, seemed to do everything in their power to diminish the otherwise impressive effects of the site on

Charles D. Robinson, *Barnard's Hotel and Cottages, c.* 1880s, oil on canvas, painting probably created as an advertisement.

the visitors staying there.[6] A retired doctor who went to Yosemite in 1876 declared that the single most expensive travel cost was food for his horses. 'During our stay in and about the Yo Semite, I paid at least $90 a ton for all the hay we needed for ten horses, and $140 a ton for barley. It was the most solemn feature of our Yo Semite life.'[7]

The valley's first hotel was a primitive 5.5 × 6-metre (18 × 20-foot) pine structure near Yosemite Falls that was housing guests by 1857. Built by four men – Judge B. S. Walworth of New York, John C. Anderson of Illinois, W. C. Walling of Pennsylvania and I. A. Epperson of Indiana – it became known as the Lower Hotel after a second hostelry was built a short distance up the valley two years later.[8] This second structure, called the 'Upper Hotel', was built by Gus Hite, a saloon-keeper from nearby Agua Fria.[9] As previously mentioned, James Mason Hutchings, who came to Yosemite in 1864, purchased the Upper Hotel for $400 and re-christened it Hutchings' Hotel for the rest of his tenancy.

At any given time there were usually two or three hotels in the valley, with inns springing up at new locations to cater to tourists. Albert Snow's Alpine House was constructed near Nevada Fall and Peregoy's Mountain View House was built at Glacier Point. There were also places to stay along the roads to the valley: Gentry's Station on the Big Oak Flat Road, the rustic Clark's Station on the Mariposa route and the more upscale Wawona Hotel, also on the latter road.

The Cosmopolitan Bathhouse and Saloon, built in 1871, was an elegant addition to the valley's tourist facilities. One customer noted that the Cosmopolitan offered the most luxurious baths and mint juleps of its day.[10] The saloon's list of 'Fancy Drinks' included champagne juleps, wine cobblers, egg nog, milk punches, brandy smashes, whiskey smashes and sangarees. (The last was a bit like modern-day sangria; it was a sweetened, iced drink of wine – or less often, ale, beer or liquor – garnished with nutmeg.) The Cosmopolitan also offered drinks named with local flair: Bridal Veil Juleps, El Capitan Cocktails and Mountaineers.

The Cosmopolitan attracted many of Yosemite's most famous visitors. Its 'Grand Register', a 61 × 46-cm (24 × 18-inch) guestbook 20 cm (8 inches) thick, was made by special order for John C. Smith, proprietor of the saloon, at a cost of $500. The Grand Register contains many illustrious signatures, including five presidents: James A.

Carleton Watkins, *Cosmopolitan Saloon*, a saloon and bath house, c. 1876, albumen photograph.

Garfield, Teddy Roosevelt, William Howard Taft, Ulysses S. Grant and Rutherford B. Hayes. Other famous visitors who signed it include Buffalo Bill Cody, General William Tecumseh Sherman, the actress Lillie Langtry, the horticulturalist Luther Burbank and Duke Alexander of Russia.[11] The Cosmopolitan closed in 1884 when the Yosemite Commission deemed it inappropriate to operate a saloon not attached to a hotel.

Many early visitors were travellers on the Grand Tour who had recently been to Italy, Switzerland and the eastern United States on their way to Hawaii and Japan. 'Here we meet tourists from the four quarters of the world', Brantz Mayer wrote in 1872: 'Britons, Germans,

Our Camp in the Yosemite Valley, near the famous Yosemite Falls, California, half of a stereograph by Underwood & Underwood, 1902.

French, Russians, South Americans, Belgians, and large numbers of our own Countrymen from the Northern and western States. There were but few wayfarers from the Middle States, and none from the Southern. The travelers were mostly of mature age, with a sprinkling of young women and very few young men.'[12] For wealthy visitors, travel itself was the important thing; Yosemite was merely one more scenic attraction, albeit a spectacular one, on the Grand Tour.

Yosemite tourists also included wealthy California residents. One writer noted in 1878 that hundreds of California businessmen spent their vacations at Yosemite every year, allowing themselves 'a spell of real gipsy life'.[13] Some San Franciscans brought along their Chinese cooks when camping, and the cooks occasionally found their way into the family's group portrait – likely an expression of status and wealth rather than a statement of familial affection. Caroline LeConte, daughter of the geologist Joseph LeConte, confided in her diary that their cook, Lee, was dissatisfied with working over a Yosemite campfire, but was 'quickly appeased by an offer of higher wages'.[14]

Wealthy Californians could afford the expense of leisure travel, but the farmers and residents of small towns in the central valley and Sierra foothills had neither the money nor the time to travel. As early as 1859 the Yosemite entrepreneur James Mason Hutchings lamented, 'it is much to be regretted that such exorbitant charges should preclude persons of limited means from visiting this magnificent valley.'[15] A letter from Anne Trescot of Hornitos, a hamlet on the Mariposa route to Yosemite, brings this economic hardship into sharp focus. Writing to her daughter Eliza around 1876, she commented: 'We are about forty miles from the valley [but] I never expect to be any nearer Mirrow [sic] Lake a trip to the valley is so expensive[.] The fare at the Hotels is enormously high.'[16]

Stagecoach roads, railroads and automobiles made travel to Yosemite faster and easier as the nineteenth century progressed and the twentieth began. In the 1870s stage roads were completed all the way to the valley floor, replacing the trails that were traversable only on horseback. Two roads were built from the west in 1874, the first from Coulterville, the second from Big Oak Flat, somewhat to the north. (These would be replaced in the twentieth century by California Highway 120.) In 1875 a third stage route, the Wawona Road, was constructed from Mariposa,

Stagecoach at Inspiration Point, Boysen Studio, *c.* 1900.

southwest of the valley, via Wawona.[17] Paved in the 1930s, and known today as Highway 41, this road now passes through the Wawona Tunnel before arriving at Inspiration Point. Every year thousands of buses decant tourists who photograph this famous vista.

Travellers usually visited the Big Trees en route. The giant sequoias had fascinated visitors from the beginning of Yosemite tourism, when they were sketched with people dancing on their immense stumps and driving carriages through their hollow trunks. The writer Mary Blake made a detour from Galen Clark's ranch on the Mariposa Trail to spend an afternoon looking at 'those freaks of nature'. Blake noted that 'A ball of twine, which you unwind for ninety or a hundred feet to measure one Grizzly Giant, *makes* you believe the size you can never understand otherwise.'[18] When President Theodore Roosevelt visited California in 1903, he was so enamoured of the Big Trees near San Francisco that he requested an additional day to tour the Mariposa Grove on his way to Yosemite.

Public fascination with the giant sequoia trees resulted in their 'commodification' by those who catered to the tourist trade. In the nineteenth century pieces of sequoia wood were sold at the groves en route to the valley. Craft objects proliferated in the nineteenth century, so that tourists could take home a piece of the Big Trees: wooden cabinets and glove-boxes, canes, tables and buttons carved of sequoia wood, even seeds from the giant sequoias.[19] Among the most peculiar Big Tree souvenirs are the elongated, vertical images of them painted by Thomas Hill on narrow planks of sequoia. One historian has commented on the irony of Hill's choice of medium. 'In a final twist of fate', she notes, 'the image and object had become one. In the most literal sense the subject of the painting had been consumed in the production of the image.'[20] Objects made of sequoia wood are no longer sold at Yosemite gift shops, although sequoia seedlings from outside the park can be purchased there.

The Southern Pacific Railroad played an important role in promoting Yosemite tourism. Following the model of the Northern Pacific, which used Yellowstone as a travel inducement, the Southern Pacific began to advertise Yosemite 'in a way that made it seem less like the remote wilderness it was and more like a gentrified wilderness made civilized by the presence of the railroad'.[21] This was deceptive advertising because the Southern Pacific stopped short of Yosemite; it went only as far as the towns in the central valley.

In 1898 the Southern Pacific Railroad began publishing *Sunset*, a magazine of 'western living' that contained fiction as well as articles on decorating, gardening and fashion. The inaugural issue featured an article about Yosemite, which had been declared a national park eight years earlier. *Sunset* has been called 'one of the most ingenious marketing strategies employed by the railroad'.[22] Named for the company's premier train, the Sunset Limited, the magazine was full of colourful advertisements for railroad travel, but the editors downplayed the fact that it was actually published by the railroad.[23] Readers could learn about the spectacular scenery of the Golden State on one page; on the next, they learned how to get there by train.

Although track was never laid into the valley itself, one rail line did bring visitors as close as El Portal, at the southwest boundary of the park. Called the Yosemite Valley Railroad, this standard-gauge, short-line railroad operated from 1907 to 1945 on track following the Merced River. Passengers disembarked at El Portal and took a stagecoach – or, beginning in 1913, a motor coach – into the valley. Among the railroad's most notable customers were two American presidents: William Howard Taft in 1909 and Franklin Delano Roosevelt in 1938.

W. H. Bull, 'Yosemite National Park', 1921, one of the Southern Pacific
Railroad's posters with a wilderness theme.

The Yosemite Valley Railroad ceased operations in 1945 due to a variety of factors: low tourist numbers during the Second World War, the closure of nearby businesses, the resulting loss of freight traffic and increased competition from automobile routes.[24]

Yosemite tourism entered a new era when the first automobile entered the valley in 1900. The first vehicle to arrive was a unique steam car called the 'Locomobile' that was owned by Oliver Lippincott of Los Angeles. Lippincott drove to Yosemite on 24 June 1900 with his mechanic, Edward Russell. After amazing residents and tourists in the valley with their vehicle, they were persuaded to drive the car up to Glacier Point Cliff. After climbing the steep, winding road for several hours, Lippincott and Russell arrived after dark and were forced to wait until morning to push the car onto the rock ledge named Overhanging Rock.

As Lippincott explained, 'Nothing would do but that the Locomobile must go out on the overhanging rock where only the most fearless and level-headed have ever dared to stand.' The men tied ropes to their waists to prevent falling off the cliff while they pushed the car as far as possible onto the rock ledge. According to Lippincott, 'The

'Locomobile' at Valley View, Yosemite Valley, 1901, the year after Oliver Lippincott drove the first such vehicle into the valley.

women buried their heads in their hands, horrified at the sight. I firmly believe that if the machine had gone over, every man of the party would have gone with it. We hung on with tooth and nail while the camera was adjusted. No picture was ever so long in being taken.'[25]

Many other visitors posed at this famous location without automobiles. One of the most famous images features Kitty Tatch and Katherine Hazelston, waitresses at the Yosemite hotels, who danced on Glacier Point Cliff in 1900. Photographs of the two girls were turned into postcards and sold for many years. The photographer Julius Boysen took a picture of a gymnast doing a handstand on Overhanging Rock in 1903. His colour lithographic postcard was titled 'Tumbler of Marvelous Nerve on Overhanging Rock'.

Beginning in 1913, the general public was permitted to drive automobiles into the park. In 1914, 127 cars entered the park; only a year later the number had reached 958 cars, carrying a total of 3,513 visitors.[26] 'Motoring' excursions were a national craze, as suggested by the formation of groups like the Auto Club of Southern California (1900), the publication of its house magazine *Touring Topics* (begun in 1909), and articles on car travel in *Sunset* and other magazines.[27] Additional evidence of the national craze can be found in young people's novels such as Katherine Stokes's *Motor Maids*, a series published between 1911 and 1914 featuring a group of young women and their adventures.

The romance of early car culture at Yosemite is perfectly summed up by *Toot Your Horn for Camp Curry*, the cover illustration of a piece of sheet music from 1915. *Toot Your Horn* depicts a stylish couple driving a bright red convertible 'roadster' up a hill, leaving the valley; behind them are El Capitan, Bridalveil Fall and Half Dome. The title makes reference to the Yosemite campground founded in 1899 by David and Jenny Curry. Glen Hood, who wrote the music and lyrics, often performed at Camp Curry.[28]

In 1916 the photographer Arthur C. Pillsbury was featured in the press when he drove his new Studebaker Six to the edge of Overhanging Rock, probably inspired by the earlier photographs of Oliver Lippincott's Locomobile. To get to Yosemite, Pillsbury drove his new car from Oakland, California, breaking the previous driving record by making the trip in less than nine hours. (Today it takes between four

George Fiske, *Danicng Girls at Glacier Point*, Kitty Tatch and Katherine
Hazelston dancing on Overhanging Rock, 1900, albumen photograph.

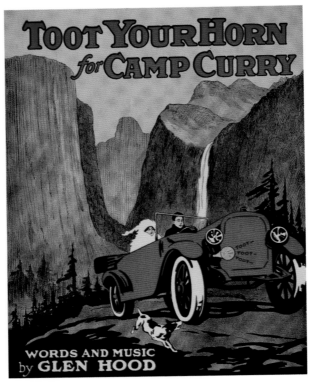

'Toot Your Horn for Camp Curry', 1915,
sheet music cover.

and five hours to drive from San Francisco to Yosemite.) Pillsbury had
a trestle built that allowed him to navigate his Studebaker over several
large rocks, stopping about a foot from the end of the cliff. His photographic postcard of his Studebaker on Overhanging Rock may be the
most famous image of this particular stunt (see p. 96).[29]

Lord James Bryce of Great Britain foresaw the dangers inherent
in making Yosemite accessible by automobile. Ambassador to the United
States from 1907 to 1913, Bryce commented, 'It would be hard to find
anywhere scenery more perfect', adding that 'If Adam had known what
harm the serpent was going to work, he would have tried to prevent
him from finding lodging in Eden; and if you were to realize what the
result of the automobile will be in that wonderful, incomparable Valley,
you will keep it out.'[30]

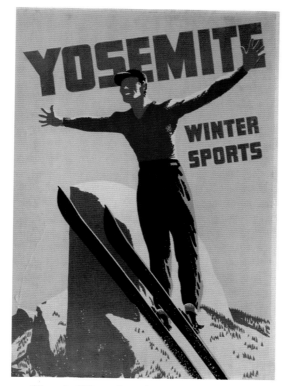

'Yosemite Winter Sports', 1930s, poster. By 1938
Yosemite was becoming 'a bustling winter mecca for the elite'.

Although Bryce's advice was good, it was insufficient to stop the tide
of tourism. With the arrival of private automobiles in 1913, tourist numbers increased, causing in turn a proliferation of roads, new buildings
and tourist amenities. The number of cars produced in the United States
more than doubled during the 1920s, resulting in nationwide expansion
of the nation's highway system.[31] At Yosemite, construction of a year-
round road into the park began in 1920, encouraged in part by the Auto
Club. That year 70 per cent of the park's 58,000 visitors arrived in private
cars.[32] Yosemite's 'all-year highway', Route 140, opened in 1926, allowing
easy access during the winter months.

As the country's highway system expanded in the 1920s, produce
and merchandise were shipped greater distances and advertising became
more national in character. Simple, eye-catching advertisements with

bright colours brought tourist imagery into the modern era. Yosemite advertising featured visitors driving cars, camping, hiking and skiing during winter vacations. The Winter Olympics, first held in 1924, may have inspired park officials and concessionaires to promote winter sports as a means of attracting tourists in the off-season. The Yosemite Park and Curry Company established the Yosemite Winter Club in 1928, along with a small ski hill and ski jump near Tenaya Creek Bridge. By 1938 Yosemite was becoming 'a bustling winter mecca for the elite'.[33]

Some of the era's most appealing advertising is found on the labels printed for crates of California fruit. Produce has little or no connection to Yosemite, but fruit crate labels helped keep the valley in the public eye, both in California and across the country. Although not created specifically as travel enticements, these labels conveyed a sense of pride in the Golden State's natural wonders. They also emphasized the more tropical aspects of California as an American Eden.

Fruit crate label, Yosemite brand, Earl Fruit Company, *c.* 1893–1909.

Carol M. Highsmith, *The Ahwahnee Hotel, Yosemite*, March 2007.

Fruit crate labels of the 1920s and early '30s were very similar to the advertisements published in *Sunset* magazine: they were easy to read and appealing, with simple, colourful images. By the 1930s California fruit growers were promoting 'Yosemite Brand', 'El Capitan', 'Half Dome', 'Bridal Veil', 'Sentinel' (with an image of Sentinel Rock), and 'National Park Brand' oranges.[34] With a Yosemite image on the National Park Brand label, the identity of the park was obvious.

Yosemite tourist facilities reached a new level of sophistication and elegance with the Ahwahnee Hotel, designed by the architect Gilbert Stanley Underwood and completed in 1927. Underwood created post office buildings and train stations, but he is best known for the lodges he built at such national parks as Yellowstone, Bryce Canyon, Grand Teton and the Grand Canyon. The Ahwahnee presented special challenges because of its remote location; over 5,000 tons of stone, 1,000 tons of steel and 30,000 feet of timber had to be hauled into the valley over mountain roads.

The Ahwahnee was probably Underwood's greatest triumph in the 'rustic style', a mode that has been called a 'natural outgrowth of a new romanticism about nature, about our country's western frontiers'.[35] Located on the valley floor and constructed of rough stone, concrete and glass, the Ahwahnee presents a picturesque appearance with its irregular shape, varied silhouette, and mix of natural and man-made materials.

Queen Elizabeth II and Prince Philip at Inspiration Point, Yosemite, 5 March 1983.

The wooden look of the hotel was actually created with concrete poured into rough wooden moulds and stained to look like redwood. Concrete construction saved the Ahwahnee from the fate of earlier Yosemite hotels that had burned down. The hotel was designated a National Historic Landmark in 1987.

The interiors of the Ahwahnee were designed by Phyllis Ackerman and Arthur Upham Pope. The Great Lounge is especially attractive, with exposed and painted beams along the ceiling, rustic chandeliers, floor-to-ceiling glass windows, carpets woven with geometric Native American patterns and dark wood Mission-style furniture. The Ahwahnee's Great Lounge has an air of rustic elegance that has kept it popular as a tourist destination over the decades.

The artist most closely affiliated with the hotel was Gunnar Widforss. A friend of Stephen Mather, first director of the National Park Service, Widforss was hired in 1927 by the Yosemite Park and Curry Company to paint watercolour views of the new Ahwahnee Hotel. Widforss's carefully articulated watercolours are well-suited to the Ahwahnee, with its varied textures and Mission-style details. Widforss's views of the hotel suggest the 'seamless blend of gorgeous nature and material luxury' that Donald Tresidder, president of the company, 'hoped his prized hotel would exude'.[36] Today framed reproductions of Widforss's watercolours are displayed on the walls of the hotel.

The Ahwahnee has seen many famous visitors over the years, including President John F. Kennedy in 1962 and Queen Elizabeth II and Prince Philip in 1983. After Queen Elizabeth's visit, the hotel's elegant 'Mary Curry Tresidder Suite' became known as 'The Queen's Room'. Other royal visitors have included King Baudouin of Belgium, Queen Ratna of Nepal and Emperor Haile Selassie of Ethiopia. The actress Lucille Ball stayed at the Ahwahnee while filming *The Long, Long Trailer* (1953), as did Mel Gibson, while he was working on *Maverick* (1994). William Shatner and Leonard Nimoy were guests in 1988 while filming scenes at Yosemite for *Star Trek V: The Final Frontier*. Other entertainers who have stayed there include Douglas Fairbanks Jr, Judy Garland, Boris Karloff, Charlton Heston, Kim Novak, Joan Baez, Robert Redford and Brad Pitt.[37]

The photographer Ansel Adams had a long working relationship with the Ahwahnee Hotel, where he helped organize the Bracebridge Dinner. A yuletide event, the dinner was first presented in 1927 – the year the hotel opened – as a means of attracting visitors in winter. Inspired by English Christmas traditions and Washington Irving's description of Squire Bracebridge, the dinner is an extravagant event with role-playing, banquet fare and costumes reminiscent of the sixteenth century. Donald Tresidder conceived the idea of the dinner and hired Garnet Holme, a California pageant director, to design the event.

Tresidder and his wife, Mary Curry Tresidder (daughter of the founders of Camp Curry), initially played the roles of Squire and Lady Brace-bridge.[38] After two years, Tresidder handed over the role of Squire to Ansel Adams, who had played the Lord of Misrule during the first two seasons.

Adams redesigned the look of the pageant, and his script for it remains largely unchanged today. He also invited the architect Theodore Spencer and his wife Jeanette Dyer Spencer to work on the project. Theodore Spencer created the set for the dinner while his wife designed

The Bracebridge Dinner at the Ahwahnee Hotel, 2012.

costumes, the stage and the head table. She was also responsible for the stained glass windows in the Great Lounge of the hotel. In 1934 Adams asked Eugene Fulton, a well-known San Francisco choral conductor, to direct the dinner's eight-member male chorus. The conductor's wife, Anna-Marie Fulton, accompanied the singers.

Although the Bracebridge Dinner is a much-loved visual, acoustic and culinary extravaganza, the event began as a marketing device un-related to the valley and its history. Adams's photographs, in contrast, are original contributions to Yosemite culture, even if they do present an idealized view of the valley. Rather than documenting Yosemite's grow-ing tourist trade, Adams focused on the natural grandeur and beauty of the valley – the seemingly unchanging physical aspects of the site. Despite Yosemite's increasing numbers of tourists, tolls, cars and camp-sites, Adams might have agreed with John Muir, who once urged a friend to visit Yosemite despite the 'desecrating influences of the fashionable hordes'. Yosemite's 'tide of visitors', wrote Muir, 'will float slowly about the *bottom* of the valley as a harmless scum, collecting in hotel and saloon eddies, leaving the rocks and falls eloquent as ever and instinct with imperishable beauty and greatness'.[39] Muir's idealized view of Yosemite's eternal beauty would be sorely tested as the twentieth century arrived, bringing increasing numbers of tourists, commercial development and environmental threats to the park.

EIGHT

Trouble in Paradise

Throughout the history of American parks, public land preservation and private interest exploitation have been in conflict, with the voices of park management, politicians, environmentalists and ordinary citizens vying for dominance. Yosemite's extreme popularity has made balancing these concerns especially difficult. From the beginning, Yosemite has been a crucible for the battle between preservation and use: that is, how to balance protecting the park's scenery and resources for future generations while making them accessible to current visitors.

When Yosemite was placed under federal control in 1906, preservationists hoped that the valley and its surroundings would finally be safe. Ironically the most bitter of all preservation battles – the fight to save Hetch Hetchy Valley – was just getting underway. Hetch Hetchy, a smaller Yosemite lookalike situated less than 20 miles northwest of Yosemite Valley, was proposed as a water source for San Francisco. The plan involved damming the Tuolumne River and flooding Hetch Hetchy as a reservoir, despite its location within the national park.

The idea of damming Hetch Hetchy was first raised in 1882, although the fight did not begin in earnest until the turn of the century. In the interim John Muir helped found the Sierra Club with the goal of protecting Yosemite and other national parks. In 1901 San Francisco mayor James Phelan filed for water rights in Hetch Hetchy. While Phelan continued his efforts to assure a dependable source of water for San Francisco, Muir and William E. Colby, secretary of the Sierra Club, launched a campaign to save the valley.[1]

To emphasize the importance of Yosemite's smaller, 'sister' valley, Muir dubbed Hetch Hetchy the 'Tuolumne Yosemite'. It was, he felt, 'a wonderfully exact counterpart of the Merced Yosemite, not only in its sublime rocks and waterfalls but in the gardens, groves and meadows of its flowery park-like floor' and in the rock walls, 'sculptured in the same style'.[2]

Once again, Muir called on his artist friends to provide visual propaganda for the cause. Travelling with the painter William Keith to Hetch Hetchy in October 1907, the naturalist was inspired to write and explore while his artist friend painted. Using his oil sketches of the area as source material, Keith created a number of Hetch Hetchy landscapes, hoping to heighten awareness of the beauties of the site. Two years later, Joseph Nisbet LeConte, son of the geologist who had sided with Muir in the glacier debate, took photographs of Hetch Hetchy to illustrate articles in the magazine *Out West*.[3] Writers, including Robert Underwood Johnson, editor of *The Century Magazine*, as well as members of the Sierra and Appalachian Trail Clubs, joined Muir in arguing against the proposal to dam Hetch Hetchy.

The range of opinions involved in the debate shows a shift in environmental thinking. John Muir, poet-naturalist of the Sierra, espoused an old-fashioned romanticism in his writings about nature. According to Muir,

Isaiah West Taber, *Hetch-Hetchy Valley Before it was Flooded*, *c.* 1908.

William Keith, *Hetch Hetchy Side Canyon I, c.* 1908, oil sketch.

These temple destroyers, devotees of ravaging commercialism, seem to have a perfect contempt for Nature, and, instead of lifting their eyes to the God of the mountains, lift them to the almighty dollar. Dam Hetch-Hetchy! As well dam for water-tanks the people's cathedrals and churches, for no holier temple has ever been consecrated by the heart of man.[4]

Gifford Pinchot, appointed the first head of the Division of Forestry (later renamed the u.s. Forest Service), took a more pragmatic and utilitarian position. Acquaintances since 1882, Muir and Pinchot both opposed reckless exploitation of natural resources. Their first major disagreement occurred in 1883, when Pinchot came out in support of sheep grazing in forest reserves. Pinchot's stand on Hetch Hetchy deepened the rift. Where Muir opposed inundating the valley's spectacular scenery, 'Pinchot countered that its beauty was of less importance than its utility as a much-needed reservoir for San Francisco.'[5] Pinchot initially had the support of President Teddy Roosevelt, although the President would have a change of heart in 1908.

The San Francisco Earthquake of 1906 and the widespread fires that followed it were factors that helped tip the balance toward flooding Hetch Hetchy and assuring an additional source of water for the city. On 11 May 1908, James R. Garfield, Secretary of the Interior, approved the city's latest request. 'Domestic use', wrote Garfield, 'is the highest use to which water and available storage basins . . . can be put.'[6]

After a long, acrimonious campaign, Muir and his supporters were forced to accept defeat when the Raker Bill was passed by Congress in 1913. Hetch Hetchy became a reservoir for San Francisco only seven years after Yosemite was made part of the national park system. Muir, whose successful battle to protect Yosemite had been the crowning achievement of his life, died the year after his failure to save Hetch Hetchy.

The conservationist Aldo Leopold, now considered the father of wildlife ecology, would take Pinchot's ideas on forest conservation in a different direction. Too young to participate actively in the Hetch Hetchy debate, Leopold graduated from the Yale University Forest School – founded through the philanthropy of the Pinchot family – in 1909. Rather than endorsing Pinchot's pragmatism, however, Leopold emphasized the importance of wilderness preservation in the National Forest system. Leopold's 'growing awareness of the interrelations of organisms and their environment led him to the realization that protecting wild country was a matter of scientific necessity as well as sentiment'.[7] Leopold became a highly effective champion of wilderness.

The United States Wilderness Act of 1964 defined wilderness as 'an area where the earth and its community of life are untrammelled by man, where man himself is a visitor who does not remain'. Although this definition still prevails among the general public, the writer Roderick Nash proposed that nature and wilderness are not entities with an absolute identity, but rather cultural constructs that change over time. William Cronon has further refined this notion. As Cronon notes, nature itself 'is a profoundly human construction' and 'the way we describe and understand [the] world is so entangled with our own values and assumptions that the two can never be fully separate.'[8]

Our understanding of wilderness, according to Cronon, has changed considerably. In the late eighteenth century, 'to be a wilderness was to be "deserted," "savage," "desolate," "barren" – in short, a "waste," the word's nearest synonym.' Today's visitors expect to find a very different version of wilderness at Yosemite and elsewhere: a landscape that seems pristine and untouched; majestic in its grander aspects (like the nineteenth-century Sublime), sylvan in its more intimate spaces (like the Picturesque).

The battle to save Hetch Hetchy was the most famous environmental crusade involving Yosemite National Park. Although the fight was ultimately lost, Hetch Hetchy became (in Cronon's words) 'the battle cry of an emerging movement to preserve wilderness'. As one of the most heavily visited sites in the u.s. National Park system, Yosemite has continued to serve as a locus for the debate about nature preservation versus park use. The problem of balancing preservation of resources with democratic access for all has no perfect solution, particularly when tourism sustains the local economy and even helps to subsidize the costs of preservation.

Concessionaires have played an important, often negative role in the development of the park. The first major concession at Yosemite began with a bakery and store established by John and Bridget Degnan in 1884. Their Desmond Park Service Company gradually built or bought out hotels, stores, camps, a dairy, a garage and other park services. David and Jenny Curry started a second concession in the valley, called the Curry Company, in 1899. The couple founded Camp Curry, a campground that is famous today for its city of over 300 'tent cabins' – shelters with wooden floors, wooden frames and canvas walls.[9]

Frederick Law Olmsted's management plan for Yosemite was squelched after it was written in 1865, but his ideas resurfaced in the twentieth century. In 1913 Acting Park Superintendent Major William T. Littlebrant requested that a board comprised of a landscape architect, a structural architect and a civil engineer formulate a new plan for improving the park. Littlebrant recommended that 'Any new constructions should be in harmony with the grandeur of the cliffs and the delicacy of the falls. The coloring of the buildings should not be in violent contrast with the grey of the rocks or the beauties of the pine and cedars.' He further urged that 'Concessioners should not be allowed to erect buildings designed by different architects without knowledge of the general plan.'[10]

Stephen Mather, appointed the first director of the National Park Service in 1917, shared Littlebrant's concerns about sympathetic

John and Bridget Degnan and their children on
the porch of their house at Yosemite, *c.* 1896.

construction and development at Yosemite. Mather established an
advisory group headed by trained architects that concerned itself with
landscape architecture and the harmonization of park structures with
their natural surroundings. The advisory group gave advice on 'engin-
eering projects and other scenic questions, such as vista-cutting'.[11]
Olmsted would have been pleased.

The Curry Company and their rival, the Yosemite National Park
Company (formerly the Desmond Park Service Company), were forced
by park management to merge in 1925, forming the Yosemite Park and
Curry Company (YPCC, afterwards generally called 'The Company').
With this merger, an entity was formed that would become a major
player at Yosemite, alternately working with and against the Park Service
in setting policy. The Company often lobbied in favour of commercial
development, promoting policies that would increase visitor capacity
and profit at the expense of the valley's natural resources. An example
occurred several years after the merger: following the repeal of Prohib-
ition in 1933, the Company successfully sought to increase the sale of
alcoholic beverages in the park. By 1988 there would be 'thirty-five outlets in Yosemite National Park selling beer, wine, or liquor, twenty-three

of those outlets on the valley floor alone'.[12] Alcoholic beverages are still among the amenities enjoyed by thousands of tourists.

As the twentieth century progressed, interactions between humans and wildlife – bears in particular – became one of Yosemite's 'hot button issues'. Photographs from the 1920s document activities no longer permitted in the park: one shows Enid Michael, a Park Service ranger, dancing with a bear; another depicts California mule deer waiting to be fed by visitors at a tent campsite.[13] When bears, overly familiar with humans, attacked campsites for food, the Yosemite Park and Curry Company favoured killing or relocating the offending animals.

It would be years before Park Service policy dictated that the best solution was to educate tourists about the proper treatment of wild animals, rather than killing animals that overstepped the bounds. Policy regarding bears first began to change in 1940, when Newton B. Drury was appointed Director of the National Park Service. Feeding the bears was discontinued at Yosemite in 1941, and the following year all national parks were ordered to cease holding bear shows. For years park regulations have forbidden campers to feed wildlife.

By mid-century Yosemite and many other national parks were suffering from a crumbling infrastructure. Many of the park's buildings, bridges, roads and trails had been constructed in the 1930s by the Civilian Conservation Corps, a New Deal employment project during the Great Depression. These facilities had deteriorated significantly by the 1950s, yet visitation increased dramatically during the same period as Americans grew more affluent and gained more leisure time in the post-war era.

To deal with these and other problems in the park, management plans have periodically been written and revised. 'Mission 66', a ten-year management plan that included upgrades and expansions of park facilities, was conceived in 1956 under Park Service Director Conrad L. Wirth.[14] Wirth's plan for Yosemite involved constructing better road and trail systems, building accommodations and facilities for visitors, and acquiring private lands for protection or use.

Some destructive practices were eliminated by management despite their celebrated status as park traditions. The potentially dangerous 'Firefall', a dramatic display of glowing coals tossed from the top of Glacier Point, came to an end in 1968 despite its popularity. The Firefall

Enid Michael, National Park Service ranger naturalist,
dancing with a bear at Yosemite National Park, *c.* 1921.

dated back to 1872, when James McCauley – proprietor of Glacier
Point Mountain House – began dumping glowing coals over the edge
of the cliff every night at 9 pm. An impressive visual spectacle, the
Firefall was celebrated over the years in brochures and other advertising as well as sheet music. It was even the name of a country-rock band
formed in 1973.

Arguing that the Firefall was not a natural phenomenon, the Park
Service banned it despite its popularity among visitors. The only Firefall nowadays is a natural lighting effect that occurs annually near the
second week of February, when the setting sun hits Horsetail Falls at
just the right angle. Previously witnessed mostly by locals and photographers who were 'in the know', this naturally occurring Firefall is
becoming better known through images posted on the Internet.

In 1970 the Park Service also stopped dredging Mirror Lake, a
practice intended to maintain the lake's famous mirror effects. To com-
pensate, small catch-dams were built upstream to keep sediment from
reaching the lake. According to one source, 'Mirror Lake has been
slowly reverting to "Mirror Meadow" ever since the park service stopped

Eadweard Muybridge, *Mirror Lake, Valley of the Yosemite*,
1872, albumen photograph.

dredging it.'[15] Mirror views now appear only in spring and early summer, when the water level is high.

One update to park policy – the introduction of controlled burning – is actually a throwback to an earlier era. When Native Americans lived in the valley, they intentionally burned undergrowth to encourage the proliferation of acorn-bearing black oaks. As soon as Anglo-Americans moved in, this practice was discontinued and the valley floor became more heavily forested. It took years for park management to understand the important role fire played in the ecology of the valley. Fire is necessary for black oak trees and also for the giant sequoia, whose seeds require fires to clear out undergrowth before they can germinate. Controlled burning is now standard practice at the park.

To protect Yosemite National Park and its ecosystem, the Park Service has periodically acquired additional lands to serve as a buffer, especially in the border areas that seem most threatened by outside interests. For example, the ten-year plan called Mission 66 encouraged the acquisition of 1,271 acres near the park. The Wilderness Act of 1964 gave wilderness status to 89 per cent of Yosemite's park lands. Yosemite National Park now measures 3,027 square kilometres (1,189 square miles). It is roughly the size of Cambridgeshire, and three-quarters the size of Rhode Island, the smallest of the United States.

Concessionaire management underwent a change in 1973 when the venerable Yosemite Park and Curry Company was acquired by the Music Corporation of America. A master plan published the following year was rejected because YPCC was seen as having undue influence in its design.[16] A General Management Plan completed in 1980 was off to a good start with five worthy goals: to reclaim priceless natural beauty; to reduce traffic congestion in the valley; to allow natural processes to prevail whenever possible; to reduce crowding; and to promote visitor understanding and enjoyment of the park. A major flood in 1997 forced the plan of 1980 into revisions. James Watt, U.S. Secretary of the Interior from 1980 to 1988, also slowed its implementation, claiming he would 'err on the side of public use versus preservation'.[17] Watt's tenure as Secretary of the Interior was a worrisome period for environmentalists.

The Yosemite concession changed hands again in 1990 when the Music Corporation of America was acquired by the Japanese conglomerate Matsushita Electric Industrial Company. After this purchase, critics complained that 'park operations should stay in American hands',[18] and negotiations began for another buyout. In 1992 the Yosemite concession was acquired by Delaware North Companies, a holding company based in Buffalo, New York, that owns racetracks and operates concession services at professional sports stadiums, arenas and airports.

Although the new contract increased Park Service revenue – 25 cents from every dollar spent in the park by visitors, instead of the previous pittance of 1 cent for every dollar – environmental issues out-ranked financial concerns when the decision was made. According to James M. Ridenour, then Director of the National Park Service, Delaware North was 'not the highest bidder monetarily', but their pro-posal 'budgeted the most money for environmental cleanup and placed no cap on its environmental mitigation responsibilities'.[19] The new arrangement also stipulated that ownership of all buildings would revert to the Park Service at the end of the fifteen-year contract.

Another Yosemite Valley Plan, proposed in 2000, was intended to 'reduce the human footprint' as much as possible, with park management continuing its efforts to limit construction, cars and visitors to the park.[20] Environmental groups criticized the new plan as being 'a development scheme veiled as restoration', however, and it was rescinded due to litiga-tion, taking park management back to the General Management Plan of 1980.[21] Those who love the park agree that change must occur, but they disagree on how it should happen. The most recent plan, targeting management of the Merced River, was released in January 2013; as usual, reactions to it vary.[22]

One effort to reduce the car problem is YARTS – the Yosemite Area Rapid Transit System – which started up in 2000. YARTS buses carry visitors and park employees into the valley along three corridors: Highway 140 eastward from Merced, Highway 120 eastward from Sonora, and Highway 120 westward through the Tioga Pass.[23] Buses also carry visitors along the valley floor loop road and to more distant destinations within the park. Limiting car traffic has been a contentious issue, with opponents claiming it would severely restrict the ability of day visitors to see the valley.

Other environmental threats have also resisted easy solutions. Al-though Yosemite flora and fauna have come under increasing protection, invasive, non-native plants present a special problem as a small percentage are highly disruptive to native flora. Two hundred species of non-native plants have been identified at Yosemite, and botanists estimate that ten more such species are identified every year. They arrive through a variety of means: seeds are carried on socks, shoelaces, vehicle tyres, backpacks and pet fur. Removal efforts are focused on nine high-priority species. Yellow star-thistle, dubbed 'one of Yosemite's most defiant players' by the National Park Service, tops the 'most wanted' list.[24] Next on the list are Himalayan blackberry, common velvet grass, Italian thistle and spotted knapweed.

Times have changed since the 1930s, when Civilian Conservation Corps workers pulled up bull thistle, common mullein and St John's wort by hand. Procedures today are based on principles of integrated pest management, and park employees have evolved an intensive plant management programme. In a summary of activities for the year 2011, the Park Service reported that it had treated 16 acres of the park with a herbicide to control yellow star-thistle.[25] Using a cherry picker, park staff can spray plants on previously unreachable, steep, unstable slopes near roadways.

New technologies have been brought to bear on Yosemite's environmental challenges. Computerized Geographic Information Systems (GIS) mapping has replaced the old vegetation maps of earlier days. Yosemite's GIS project, begun in 1997, allows park employees to view and map vegetation as 'ecological communities' instead of 'clumps of large trees'. This advance allows much more refinement in plant management. For example, areas identified in the 1930s as ponderosa pine are mapped today as 'ponderosa pine with mountain misery, or with shrubs, or with grass, or with no understory (leaf litter). Ecologically, these different types of ponderosa pine communities behave differently.'[26]

Despite its location in the mountains, Yosemite receives its share of air pollution. The valley is 'downwind of many air pollution sources, including agriculture, industry, major highways, and urban pollutants from as far away as the San Francisco Bay Area'.[27] Westerly winds blow that pollution into the park, where it can affect natural and scenic resources. Yosemite's park management, in cooperation with state and federal agencies, monitors and works to improve air quality in the park.

Yellow star-thistle (*Centaurea solstitialis*), which tops the 'most wanted'
list of Yosemite's invasive, non-native plants.

RECENT EVENTS AT YOSEMITE mirror on a small scale the broader
currents moving through American society. A low point in Yosemite's
history occurred during the summer of 1970 with an event called the
Stoneman Meadow Riot. A large number of young people gathered in
the park, many of them camping illegally in Stoneman Meadow, a
grassy area near the eastern end of the valley. Park rangers' efforts to
evict the illegal campers resulted in riots, with the campers throwing
rocks at the rangers and pulling them from their horses. The event
ended with 30 individuals hospitalized and 135 arrested.[28] The National
Guard was brought in to restore order.

A young park ranger named Thomas A. Smith had just started his
career at the time of the riot. According to Smith, the Park Service
learned 'the hard way' that rangers who had studied only forestry and park
management could not cope with situations like riots. Smith described

Half Dome traffic on the Cables Route before the current permit system.

Yosemite as being 'like a small mobile city, with twenty thousand people or more in any given day'. The General Authorities Act of 1976 gave park rangers the power to carry firearms and investigate crime. As a national park, federal laws apply at Yosemite. 'Neither the Highway Patrol nor the local sheriff [has] jurisdiction inside the Park.'[29]

At the end of the twentieth century several crises alarmed visitors and caused a temporary decrease in tourism. In 1999 a large rockslide originated at the east side of Glacier Point and deposited debris over an area larger than several football fields. That same year, a disturbed young man killed three female visitors staying in El Portal, just outside the park, and another woman living in Foresta, within the park borders. Despite these upsetting and violent events, tourism suffered for only a short time.

The power of nature reminds us that we explore at our own risk. The year 2011 was one of the most dangerous in Yosemite's recent history, with eighteen deaths having occurred in the park by early September. These included three hikers who were swept over the 97-metre (317-foot) Vernal Falls when one fell in and the others attempted a rescue; another who slipped and fell into the Merced River while hiking the Mist Trail; two hikers who drowned in Hetch Hetchy Reservoir; a woman who fell to her death while descending Half Dome along the popular cables route; and a 23-year-old man who fell from the face of Half Dome.[30]

In an effort to control crowds and ensure visitor safety along the cables route, the Park Service has expanded the hiking permit system from weekends to seven days a week. Park management has also instituted a new lottery system intended to eliminate 'scalping' – the resale of hiking tickets at a significantly higher price.[31] In what must often seem an impossible task, Yosemite's park management continues to search for an acceptable balance between park preservation, visitor safety and democratic access for all.

NINE

A National Playground

The Park Service experienced a 'moment of truth' on 31 December 1954, when the total number of tourists who had visited Yosemite during the preceding calendar year topped one million. It seemed that Frederick Law Olmsted, Yosemite's first outspoken proponent of preservation, was vindicated in his prophecy that 'in a century the whole number of visitors will be counted by the millions.'[1] Tourist numbers topped 2 million in 1967, 3 million in 1987, and 4 million in 1994. A record 4,047,880 visitors went to the park in 1996, a number not repeated until 2011.[2]

Today's Yosemite devotees are as passionate about the valley as John Muir was, and like tourists of the nineteenth century, they come for a variety of reasons. 'Hardcore' wilderness fans hike and camp remote trails in the Sierra Nevada, scorning the overpopulated valley floor. Thousands nevertheless stay in the valley every year in tents, cabins, camper-trailers and hotels. Rock climbers rappel Yosemite's cliffs, while hang gliders float from rock promontories to the valley floor. Honeymooning couples and entire wedding parties stay in the valley, and weddings are performed at a variety of locations. Artists, both amateur and professional, continue to find inspiration in Yosemite's 'weird Beauty and terrible Grandeur'.

The Park Service website has a long list of 'Things To Do' at Yosemite: hiking, biking, backpacking, horse riding, birdwatching, picnicking, rock climbing, fishing, summer and winter sports, and attending ranger talks and interpretive programmes. There are hiking and biking tours of the valley itself, and hiking tours to more distant locations in the park, with trails rated easy, moderate or strenuous. Nearly 95 per cent of the park is designated 'wilderness' – a special distinction

Snowboarder at Badger Pass ski resort, Yosemite.

granted by Congress to protect the land from further development. Within Yosemite's 2,850 square kilometres (1,100 square miles) of wilderness there are over 1,200 kilometres (750 miles) of trail. Hunting is not allowed, however, and poachers are prosecuted.

The valley floor doesn't usually receive enough snow for skiing and snowboarding, but fans of those sports can visit Badger Pass, located on the road to Glacier Point. Established in 1935, Badger Pass is the oldest downhill ski resort in California. Yosemite's winter sports also include cross-country skiing, snowshoeing and ice-skating at the rink in Curry Village. Some visitors enjoy backpacking in winter, which often requires skis or snowshoes and camping in the snow. Winter trails are located at Badger Pass, Crane Flat and the Mariposa Grove of Big Trees.

Summer sports are even more numerous and include swimming, fishing, boating and rafting. There are outdoor pools at Curry Village and Yosemite Lodge, and swimming is permitted in all bodies of water except Hetch Hetchy Reservoir and above waterfalls. Swimming in the Merced River comes with warnings about swift currents, cold water and hazards such as trees and rocks in the river. Rafts can be rented for use in the Merced; visitors may also bring their own non-motorized vessels such as rafts, kayaks and canoes.

It might come as a surprise that there are regulations for picnicking, but wild animals make such rules necessary. The park website warns that 'Yosemite is home to black bears, mule deer, mountain lions, and hundreds of other species. Bears are quick learners, have a powerful sense of smell, and seek out food where it can easily be found. If a bear obtains human food, it may learn to return for more.' Park management recommends that picnickers keep their distance from animals, never feed wild animals and dispose of trash in bear-proof trash cans or dumpsters. If a bear approaches, tourists are advised to 'yell as loudly as possible to scare the bear away.'

Visitors can sign up for guided mule rides as well as pack and saddle trips in the valley, at Wawona and at Tuolumne Meadows. Visitors may bring their own horses and arrange boarding with the park concessionaire, DNC Parks & Resorts. When picketed, horses must be tied so they cannot chew on tree bark or eat the leaves of woody vegetation. Curiously, llamas are specifically banned from certain trails unless the riders obtain written permission from the park superintendent.

Hang gliding and BASE jumping are among the most dramatic sports at Yosemite. Hang gliding is legal, and there is even a Yosemite Hang Gliding Association – a chapter of the national organization – that oversees gliding activities in the park. Many of those who hang glide

Bride on a snowboard at Badger Pass, Yosemite.

from the walls of the valley to the fields below post videos of their flights on YouTube and Vimeo. BASE jumping, which involves a small, initially closed parachute or a wingsuit, is now illegal in the valley, as a few BASE jumpers have died there. (The name comes from the four structures usually involved: buildings, antennas, spans or bridges, and earth or cliffs.) Ironically BASE jumping may have received its first widespread publicity at Yosemite when its founder, Carl Boenish, jumped off El Capitan in August 1978.[3] Despite the efforts of park management to stop BASE jumpers, enthusiasts have continued to practice their sport at Yosemite, sometimes with disastrous results.[4]

Rock climbing is another dramatic, high-visibility sport at Yosemite, with Half Dome and El Capitan providing the valley's most famous climbing walls. Half Dome was first climbed in 1875 by George G. Anderson, who 'drilled his way up' the rock, 'about 1,500 feet in two days'.[5] Using the rings and ropes Anderson attached, Sallie Dutcher – Carleton Watkins's photographic assistant – was the first woman to make the ascent later the same year. Rock climbers love their sport because of the challenges it presents; they enjoy researching each new climb and testing their own endurance and physical abilities.

When this book was first begun, a real-life father/daughter team climbed the face of Half Dome using ropes and the metal rings already anchored in the granite. California resident Jim Herson and his twelve-year-old daughter Kara climbed most of the cliff the first day and stopped to bivouac overnight on a ledge known as 'Big Sandy'. Herson's entertaining, affectionate account of their adventure describes the 'poop tube' Kara decorated for use during the climb and the dry, nearly inedible cactus tortillas they ate for dinner.[6]

In January 2015, as this book neared completion, two professional rock climbers – Tommy Caldwell and Kevin Jorgeson – were the first to 'free climb' El Capitan's Dawn Wall, called the 'holy grail' of big wall climbing in the United States. Over nineteen days, the pair inched up the cliff face using only their chalked hands and sticky rubber shoes. They wore harnesses and ropes for safety only, and set up base camp in three 'portaledges' – flat-bottomed tents attached to the rock wall – where they rested, allowed their fingers to heal and slept at night.

The most popular means of ascending Half Dome is by way of the Cables Route, following roughly along the course George Anderson established in 1875. Hikers start from the valley floor near Happy Isles and continue beyond Vernal and Nevada Falls. The 11-kilometre (7-mile) walk around the back of Half Dome ascends nearly a mile from the valley floor. The final 122-metre (400-foot) ascent utilizes two steel cables that serve as handholds on the northeast shoulder of the Dome. The first cables at this location were installed in 1919. Before a permit system was implemented in 2010, the lines of people ascending by the Cables resembled shopping queues at Christmas, so heavily populated was this route up the Dome.[7] More than 1,200 hikers went up on busy weekend days. Permits now limit the number to 400 hikers a day, although the system was being reassessed even as this book was written.

Half Dome inspires great devotion among rock climbers. One of the rock's biggest fans, Rick Deutsch, published a book about Half Dome containing a history of the climb and recommendations for those attempting it.[8] At the time of writing, he has made 40 trips up the rock. Deutsch – also known as 'Mr Half Dome' – claims that most people in good condition can hike the Cables Route given sufficient education, preparation and motivation. 'The secrets', he says, 'are good boots, rubberized gloves, hiking poles, and staying hydrated'. Deutsch warns against the practice of clipping oneself to the cables: 'falling while wearing a home-made system can snap your back since it has no give if you fall.' He also warns climbers to avoid the hike entirely if there is rain or stormy weather moving in.[9]

Five young men who climbed Half Dome in 1985 learned the importance of such recommendations to their dismay. They started up Half Dome late in the day, despite the strong possibility of inclement weather and warnings from other hikers, and when a storm began, they took shelter in the rock enclosure at the summit. Lightning struck the Dome twice, killing one hiker instantly and causing a second to fall over the edge of the cliff. Two of the three survivors were badly injured. Hikers who arrived at the scene later that evening administered emergency medical treatment until an air ambulance helicopter arrived at 12:30 am. The helicopter made three dangerous trips to the top of the Dome and brought the survivors down from the summit.[10]

For less adventurous visitors, park rangers offer walking tours of the valley, summer bus tours in open-air trams and enclosed bus tours during winter. Buses also carry tourists to Glacier Point, Tuolumne Meadows and the Mariposa Grove of giant sequoias. Despite the fact that park management hopes to reduce the number of automobiles entering Yosemite, touring in private cars remains popular. All roads in the park offer wonderful scenery, but the most famous scenic drive is the Tioga Road, a 63-kilometre (39-mile) route from Crane Flat to Tioga Pass that is typically open from late May or early June into November.

Yosemite Valley has been a wedding and honeymoon destination since the first Anglo-American tourists began to visit. A 'lady correspondent' of 1858 mentioned seeing 'two or three wedding parties' in the valley that summer.[11] One was probably the Ralston-Fry wedding party – the first celebrity couple to choose Yosemite for their honeymoon destination. The groom, William C. Ralston, would become one of the wealthiest men in California banking before his untimely death in 1875. The bride, Lizzie Fry, was the adopted daughter of John D. Fry, a member of the Illinois legislature who had moved to California. After their wedding on 20 May 1858, their entire wedding party accompanied them to the valley.[12]

Hang glider at Yosemite, with Half Dome in the background.

Tommy Caldwell 'free climbing' the Dawn Wall of El Capitan, 2013.
Caldwell and Kevin Jorgeson completed the first free climb
of the entire 'Dawn Wall' on 15 January 2015.

Another notable Yosemite wedding involved Harry Cassie Best, a painter who visited Yosemite in 1901, fell in love with a young woman from Los Angeles named Sarah Anne Ripley, and married her that very summer. Their wedding was held, appropriately, at the foot of Bridalveil Fall. The groom applied to the Yosemite commissioners for a permit to sell paintings and photographs, and the following spring opened his first gallery and studio in the valley.[13] One of Best's most famous patrons was President Teddy Roosevelt, who acquired a painting during his 1903 visit.

Best's daughter Virginia carried on the family tradition by celebrating her own wedding in the valley. She married photographer Ansel Adams at her father's studio in 1928. Because they married impetuously after a three-day engagement, the bride wore her best dress, which happened to be black, and the groom was attired in a jacket and tie, plus fours and black basketball sneakers.[14] Friends politely photographed him from the waist up, avoiding the more embarrassing elements of his outfit.

Yosemite is immensely popular today as a wedding destination. Weddings are performed at the Yosemite Chapel, the Ahwahnee Hotel and a variety of outdoor locations. Photo shoots range in location from the valley floor to Glacier Point Cliff and the top of Sentinel Dome. The valley's popularity, its religious associations and the Christianized pantheism so widespread in California all play a role in its continuing popularity as a wedding site.

Those interested in arranging a Yosemite wedding can look up application procedures on the Internet, where several ministers and photographers advertise their services. Posing with Yosemite Falls or Bridalveil Fall in the background is just as popular today as it was a century ago. The Ahwahnee Hotel offers weddings on the lawn with Yosemite Falls as the backdrop. Couples who get married at the Yosemite Chapel can pose with either Yosemite Falls or Half Dome behind them.

Photographers have been able to take workshops and classes at Yosemite taught by leading landscape and nature photographers ever since 1940, when Virginia and Ansel Adams started the tradition. Recent workshops have included week-long sessions such as 'Ansel Adams' Yosemite: The Art of Seeing', 'Full Moon Night Photography', 'Yosemite in Autumn: A New View', and 'Fine Art Digital Printing'.[15] Historic and alternative processes such as platinum-palladium printing and the gum bichromate process are also available, and photographers come from all over the country to participate. The Ansel Adams Gallery exhibits and sells work by a wide range of photographers, while the Yosemite Museum displays art exhibitions during spring and summer. For the general public, free photography walks are offered throughout the year and free art classes are available at the Yosemite Art and Education Center.

For serious artists, the Yosemite Renaissance organization offers an artist-in-residence programme and a series of annual art exhibitions. The exhibitions, held in the park since 1986, are open to artists working in a range of media and styles, although the subject-matter is limited to work based on the 'landscape, environment, wildlife and people of Yosemite or the environment of the Sierra'.[16] Diverse interpretations are encouraged.

The Yosemite Renaissance exhibitions are organized by an independent group of curators, artists and administrators whose goals are 'to bring together the works of serious contemporary artists that do not simply duplicate traditional representations; to establish a continuum

Bride and groom at the Yosemite Chapel, with Yosemite Falls in the background.

with past generations of Yosemite artists; and to help re-establish visual art as a major interpretive medium of the landscape and a stimulus to the protection of the environment'. The organizers note that painting and photography played an important role in establishing the national park, and they hope that art will be 'just as important in future efforts to preserve and protect that heritage'.

Artists today are challenged to find a place for themselves within a multicultural, pluralist art world. As might be expected, contemporary artists' responses to Yosemite have varied widely. Painters' interpretations have ranged from the realistic to the abstract, with a wide range

Gregory Kondos, *Half Dome*, 1993, oil on canvas.

of styles in between. Two leading California artists, Wayne Thiebaud and Gregory Kondos, have translated the beauties of nature into the glories of paint. Using brushes thickly loaded with pigment, Thiebaud and Kondos delineate simple forms like Half Dome, El Capitan, Yosemite Falls, and the steep rock walls of the valley in rich, luscious colours. The internationally recognized Pop artist David Hockney has made both paintings and photographs of Yosemite landscapes – the former in bright, semi-abstract shapes, the latter using a Cubist-inspired photo-collage method. In 2011 Hockney's photographic piece *Merced River, Yosemite Valley* brought $40,000 in an auction at Christie's New York.[17] More recently, this 'early adopter' of new technology has created colourful Yosemite landscapes using an iPad, the 'Brushes' app, a stylus and a digital inkjet printer.[18]

The British artist Tony Foster paints recognizable landscapes and attaches small plants, rocks and other items found at the locations in the images. Foster has written of the spiritual component of nature and its place in his work, commenting:

> all societies need to express their reverence for extraordinary places. Tribal societies express this admiration through their religious practices and ceremonies. Our own, more secular society, expresses it by designating National and State Parks, National Forests and Monuments, thus rendering them sacrosanct. It

David Hockney, *Merced River, Yosemite Valley*, September 1982, photographic collage.

Tony Foster, *Eight Days on Eagle Peak – Looking East*, 2005, watercolour and pencil on paper with map, wood, rocks, pinecone and other nature samples.

could be argued that the Environmental Movement is the secular means by which we express our need to honour the Earth.[19]

One team of photographers has paid the ultimate compliment to earlier Yosemite artists by incorporating those images into their own. For their *Four Views from 'Panorama Rock'*, Mark Klett and Bryan Wolfe took their own photographs, aligning the images perfectly with two mammoth plate prints from 1872 by Eadweard Muybridge.[20] The resulting work serves as both a new interpretation of the site and a homage to one of Yosemite's pioneer artists.

Some of the most interesting contemporary photographers have focused on the ironic aspects of human interactions with nature, rather than the beauties of the scenery. As one writer notes, Ansel Adams's famous *Clearing Winter Storm, Yosemite National Park* finds its near opposite in Roger Minick's *Woman with Scarf at Inspiration Point, Yosemite National Park*, taken about 40 years later.[21] Adams captured

Ted Orland, *One-and-a-Half Domes*, 1976, hand-coloured gelatin silver print.

Roger Minick, 'Woman with Scarf at Inspiration Point, Yosemite National Park', from the *Sightseer* series, 1980, chromogenic colour print.

sublime, unpopulated scenery; Minick focused on a tourist wearing a souvenir scarf, standing in front of a panoramic vista like those printed on the scarf. The former inspires an appreciation of nature's grandeur; the latter evokes a chuckle.

Ted Orland has worked at Yosemite over the course of many years, creatively capturing both its majestic scenery and its humorous side. Orland's *One-and-a-Half Domes*, which depicts the famous formation as seen from Glacier Point, includes two additional 'Half Domes' – one a two-dimensional image on a sign, the other a curved trash can hood – thus achieving the number of domes referenced in the title. Bruce Davidson, a New York City-based photographer better known for urban imagery, photographed Yosemite campgrounds in 1966. The most famous image of the series, *Camp Ground No. 4, Yosemite National Park*, depicts a wooded campground full of camper-trailers and overweight tourists in lawn chairs. The image is more ironic than humorous, conveying how suburban the park looks when populated by tourists who bring their creature comforts to the wilderness.

Although photographs like Davidson's seem to highlight all that is wrong about the park today, the campers in his image are clearly enjoying the valley in their own way. Yosemite visitors find their own

Mark Klett and Byron Wolfe, *Four Views from 'Panorama Rock,' an Obscure Outcrop off the Panorama Cliff Trail: Two Re-photographs, a Speculation on Muybridge's Missing Plate No. 39, and Another Photograph Added to the Left*, 2002, digital inkjet print. Right two panels: Eadweard Muybridge, *Cloud's Rest. Valley of the Yosemite. No. 40*, and *Glacier Channels. Valley of the Yosemite. From Panorama Rock. No. 41*, 1872 (combined to form overlapping views).

balance of nature and comfort. The vast majority camp in tents, cabins and tent-cabins on the valley floor, or relax more comfortably in hotels within the park and motels outside its borders. The many tent-cabins at Curry Village resemble a kind of 'wilderness city'. Campers at Curry Village may find themselves painfully aware of their neighbours, from the infants and small children who wake early in the morning to the teenagers and young adults who carouse late at night.

According to the Park Service, 'Unrestricted camping is no longer allowed in Yosemite Valley because of the damage it causes. The place-ment of campgrounds and campsites has changed . . . in response to a growing understanding of river dynamics, geologic hazards, and the park's natural and cultural resources.'[22] The total number of campsites was reduced after the rockfall of 2008, for example, although some were later replaced by new campsites elsewhere in the valley.

Another sign of Yosemite's popularity is its continued 'commod-ification' in the form of souvenirs – a practice that has expanded

Bruce Davidson, *Camp Ground No. 4, Yosemite National Park*,
1966, gelatin silver print.

exponentially with the growth of the Internet. Souvenirs of the valley
can be purchased online as well as on site; they take the form of T-shirts,
hats, coffee mugs, compact discs, computer mouse-pads and a variety
of other products. In the valley visitors can buy everything from postcards to the fine art sold in the Ansel Adams Gallery. Some tourists
spend a significant part of their time watching videos of the scenery
around them, rather than looking at the scenery itself.

One of the most unusual examples of commodification – or perhaps
of a truce between conservation and commercialization – occurred in
1969, when Ansel Adams's *Winter Morning, Yosemite Valley, California*
was printed in sepia tones on thousands of Hills Bros. coffee cans. In
this usage, Adams's image suggests that Hills Bros. coffee has the fresh
flavour and robust strength needed on a frigid mountain morning.
Adams himself wrote that the coffee can, one of his last commercial
jobs, had seemed 'potentially corny' but was 'actually reasonable', with
thousands of 3-lb cans of coffee sold nationwide in grocery stores for
$2.35 each. The popularity of both Yosemite Valley and Ansel Adams's
photography is such that these coffee cans have become collectibles;
they sell for up to $1,500 at auction.[23]

In 1973 Adams also participated in a television advertisement for the Datsun car company, which showed him standing next to a Datsun while photographing a forest. Defending his participation in this merchandising of the American wilderness, Adams explained that he chose 'to have images reproduced on behalf of the cause I believe in: creative photography and environmental protection'.[24] To the credit of the car company, their ad campaign included a conservation component: 'for every person who test-drove a Datsun, the u.s. Forest Service planted a tree'.[25]

Hills Bros. coffee can decorated with sepia photograph of Ansel Adams's *Winter Morning, Yosemite Valley, California*, 1969.

Yosemite Valley continues to appear in television and print ads, music videos and feature films. In a music video from 1987 the rock musician David Lee Roth was shown climbing Yosemite's rock walls; the final scene shows him standing atop a pinnacle known as Lost Arrow. The renowned photographer Galen Rowell took the album's cover shot, in which Roth rappels the face of Half Dome. Print and TV advertisements have used Yosemite as the backdrop for everything from hiking gear to men's underwear. In October 2014, Apple Inc. released the OS X Yosemite operating system for Macintosh computers; beneath a forbidding image of El Capitan's sheer face looming through snow and clouds appears the tag line 'Every bit as powerful as it looks.' Whether appearing as the background for an album cover or lending its name and its unmistakable granite walls to computer software, the valley continues to embody strength and enduring beauty.

Images of Yosemite also continue to convey religious and nationalistic associations. In Terry Gilliam's futuristic film *Twelve Monkeys* (1995), the main character, James Cole (played by Bruce Willis), is sent back in time to stop a pandemic that will wipe out 99 per cent of the earth's population. When Cole returns to his own present day, he is given psychological examinations by a team of doctors who strap him to a hospital bed; above his bed is Bierstadt's dramatic landscape *Sunset in Yosemite Valley*. In this context, the painting conveys a message about the restorative powers of nature in a dystopian future where direct experience of nature could be fatal.

The fifth Star Trek movie, *The Final Frontier* (1989), begins with a vacation sequence set in Yosemite Valley, where Captain Kirk (played by William Shatner) climbs the sheer face of El Capitan while his companions relax at their campsite. Kirk's climb is cut short when his Vulcan science officer, Mr Spock (Leonard Nimoy), ascends in rocket boots to summon Kirk back to their starship. On the evidence of *Star Trek V: The Final Frontier* – and the millions of visitors who arrive every year – it appears that Yosemite will exercise its hold on our imaginations and draw visitors to its scenic wonders for centuries to come.

References

1 GRANITE PLUTONS AND 'GOD'S GREAT PLOW'

1 John S. Hittell [1868] quoted in James Mason Hutchings, *In the Heart of the Sierras: The Yo Semite Valley, Both Historical and Descriptive; and Scenes by the Way* (Oakland, CA, 1886), p. 15.
2 For names see Peter Browning, *Place Names of the Sierra Nevada* (Berkeley, CA, 1986).
3 Beverly R. Ortiz and Julia F. Parker, *It Will Live Forever: Traditional Yosemite Indian Acorn Preparation* [1991] (Berkeley, CA, 1996), p. 2.
4 Browning, *Place Names of the Sierra Nevada*, pp. 26, 158, 227.
5 Craig D. Bates and Martha J. Lee, *Tradition and Innovation: A Basket History of the Indians of the Yosemite–Mono Lake Area* (Yosemite, CA, 1990), p. 19.
6 Ibid. See also Alfred Runte, *Yosemite: The Embattled Wilderness* (Lincoln, NE, 1990), p. 12.
7 Allen F. Glazner and Greg M. Stock, *Geology Underfoot in Yosemite National Park* (Missoula, MT, 2010), pp. 4–6.
8 Ibid.
9 Information courtesy Michael J. Hozik, Professor of Geology, Stockton University, Galloway, New Jersey.
10 George Wuerthner, *Yosemite: A Visitor's Companion* (Mechanicsburg, PA, 1994), pp. 54–8.
11 Eugene P. Kiver and David V. Harris, *Geology of U.S. Parklands* (New York, 1999), p. 221.
12 Glazner and Stock, *Geology Underfoot*, pp. 6–9, 18ff.
13 Charles C. Gillispie, *Genesis and Geology: A Study in the Relations of Scientific Thought, Natural Theology, and Social Opinion in Great Britain, 1790–1850* (New York, 1959), chapters Four and Five.

14 Josiah D. Whitney, *Geology of California*, vol. 1: *Report of Progress and Synopsis of the Field-work, From 1860 to 1864* (Philadelphia, PA, 1865), pp. 421–2.

15 Michael L. Smith, *Pacific Visions: California Scientists and the Environment, 1850–1915* (New Haven, CT, 1987), pp. 100–102.

16 William H. Goetzmann, *Exploration and Empire: The Explorer and the Scientist in the Winning of the American West* (New York, 1978), p. 371.

17 Clarence King, 'Field Notes and Observations on The Yosemite Valley and Surrounding Country', October–November 1864, MSS, n.p., Hague Collection, Box 2, Huntington Library, San Marino, California.

18 Quoted in Neil E. Fahy, 'Josiah D. Whitney, The California State Geological Survey, and Yosemite Valley', *California Geology*, XXXVIII/6 (June 1985), p. 132.

19 Sarah A. J. Locke (Smith), 'Diary of Events for a Trip to Yo Semite, June 5–21, 1879', entries for 9, 10 and 11 June, typescript, pp. 5–7, Yosemite Research Library, Yosemite, California.

20 John Muir, *My First Summer in the Sierra* (Boston, MA, and New York, 1911), p. 211.

21 François E. Matthes, *Geologic History of the Yosemite Valley* (U.S. Geological Survey Professional Paper No. 160, 1930).

22 N. King Huber, *The Geologic Story of Yosemite National Park* (Washington, DC, 1987).

23 Greg M. Stock et. al., 'High-resolution Three-dimensional Imaging and Analysis of Rock Falls in Yosemite Valley, California', *Geosphere*, VII/2 (April 2011), pp. 573–81.

24 'Ahwiyah Point Rockfall Estimated', www.nps.gov, accessed 29 July 2011. Additional information courtesy Greg Stock, Yosemite National Park.

25 'Rock Fall' and 'Highway 120 Big Oak Flat Road Closed in Yosemite National Park', www.nps.gov, accessed 18 February 2012.

26 'Yosemite National Park – Plants', www.nps.gov, accessed 13 March 2014.

27 'Yosemite National Park – Vegetation Species List – Lodgepole Pine Factoid', www.nps.gov, accessed 12 January 2014.

28 John Muir, *The Yosemite* (New York, 1912), pp. 149–50.

29 'Park Planning Calendar: Did You Know?', www.nps.gov, accessed 5 August 2012.

30 'Yosemite National Park – Habitats and Vegetation', www.digital-desert.com, accessed 12 January 2013.

31 John H. Burde and George A. Feldhamer, *Mammals of the National Parks: Conserving America's Wildlife and Parklands* (Baltimore, MD, 2005), pp. 95, 119.

32 Alfred Runte, *Yosemite: The Embattled Wilderness* (Lincoln, NE, 1990), p. 174.

33 David Braun, 'Yosemite Black Bears Target Minivans for Food Raids', *National Geographic* (15 October 2009), www.newswatch .nationalgeographic.com, accessed 30 September 2013. Article cites *Journal of Mammalogy* (October 2009).

34 'Yosemite National Park – Mountain Lions', www.nps.gov, accessed 30 September 2013.

35 'Yosemite National Park – Mammals', www.nps.gov, accessed 13 August 2012.

36 'Yosemite National Park – Birdwatching', www.nps.gov, accessed 10 August 2012.

2 DISCOVERY: WEIRD BEAUTY AND TERRIBLE GRANDEUR

1 John C. Ewers, ed., *Adventures of Zenas Leonard, Fur Trader* (Norman, OK, 1959), p. 79.

2 William Penn Abrams, 'Diary, 1849–51', manuscript, n.p., Bancroft Library, University of California at Berkeley.

3 Lafayette Houghton Bunnell, *Discovery of the Yosemite, and the Indian War of 1851, Which Led to That Event* (Chicago, IL, 1880), pp. 14ff.

4 Ibid., p. 14.

5 Stephen Powers, *Tribes of California* (Washington, DC, 1877), p. 361.

6 Peter E. Palmquist and Thomas R. Kailbourn, *Pioneer Photographers of the Far West: A Biographical Dictionary, 1840–1865* (Stanford, CA, 2000), p. 313.

7 Helen Hunt Jackson, *Bits of Travel at Home* (Boston, MA, 1890), p. 108.

8 James Mason Hutchings, 'Diary', entry for 11 June 1855, typed copy, p. 94, Yosemite Research Library, Yosemite, California.

9 Hank Johnston, *The Yosemite Grant, 1864–1906: A Pictorial History* (Yosemite, CA, 1995), p. 29.

10 Hutchings, 'Diary', entry for 17 July 1855, pp. 105, 108.

11 Hutchings, 'Diary', entries for 26 June–30 July 1855, pp. 99–112.

12 Joseph Hutchinson, letter to his father, 7 June 1859, typed copy, p. 14, Yosemite Research Library.

13 'Stereoscopic Views of the Yosemite', San Francisco *Daily Times*, X/84 (19 August 1859), p. 3.

14 Naomi Rosenblum, *A World History of Photography* [1984], 3rd edn (New York, 1997), pp. 650–51.

15 Thomas C. Roche, 'Correspondence. Yosemite Valley, June 10, 1871', *Anthony's Photographic Bulletin*, II/20 (August 1871), p. 269.

16 Erin H. Turner, *More than Petticoats: Remarkable California Women* (Guilford, CT, 1999), p. 60.

17 Jackson, *Bits of Travel at Home*, p. 108.

18 Callie, 'The Switzerland of America', *Union County Herald*, typed copy, p. 6, Yosemite Research Library.

19 Turner, *More than Petticoats*, p. 61.

20 James D. Smillie, 'Diaries', entry for 2 July 1871, microfilm (roll 2849, frame 1215), Archives of American Art, New York.

21 W. E. Dennison, comp., 'Information for the Use of Yosemite Visitors' (Sacramento, CA, 1886), booklet, p. 9. Warshaw Collection, Photographic History Division, National Museum of American History. Dennison was Yosemite Guardian from 1884 to 1887.

22 Brantz Mayer quoted Whitney in a letter to his wife, Cornelia Poor Mayer, 17 June 1872, pp. 1–2, Huntington Library, San Marino, California.

23 Copyright no. 2765 (21 March 1872), Allen & Ellis of Cincinnati; and Copyright no. 2088 (21 February 1874), W. H. Oakley, Jr of New York; Library of Congress, Washington, DC.

24 Herbert L. Aulls, 'Over Foot Trails and Bridle Paths to Yo-Semite', 1876, manuscript, Denver Public Library, Colorado, p. 60.

3 YOSEMITE AS HOME

1 Mark David Spence, *Dispossessing the Wilderness: Indian Removal and the Making of the National Parks* (New York and Oxford, 1999), p. 103.

2 Craig D. Bates and Martha J. Lee, *Tradition and Innovation: A Basket History of the Indians of the Yosemite-Mono Lake Area* (Yosemite, CA, 1990), p. viii.

3 Galen Clark, *Indians of the Yosemite Valley and Vicinity* (Yosemite, CA, 1904), p. 76.

4 Frank La Pena, Craig D. Bates and Stephen P. Medley, comps, *Legends of the Yosemite Miwok* [1981] (Yosemite, CA, 1993), p. 81.

5 James Mason Hutchings, 'The Great Yo-Semite Valley', *Hutchings' California Magazine*, IV/5 (November 1859), pp. 197–9.

6 La Pena, Bates and Medley, *Legends of the Yosemite Miwok*, pp. 41–2.

7 Ibid., pp. 37–8.

8 S. A. Barrett and E. W. Gifford, 'Miwok Material Culture: Indian Life of the Yosemite Region', *Bulletin of the Public Museum of the City of Milwaukee*, II/4 (March 1933), p. 137.

9 Ibid., pp. 140–43, 146. Additional information courtesy Brian Bibby.

10 Ibid., pp. 198, 205.

11 Edward Curtis, *The North American Indian*, vol. XIV (Seattle, WA, published serially 1907–30), p. 133.

12 Spence, *Dispossessing the Wilderness*, p. 104.

13 Brian Bibby, 'Native American Art of the Yosemite Region', *Yosemite: Art of an American Icon*, exh. cat., Autry National Center (Los Angeles, CA, 2006), p. 93.

14 Constance Gordon-Cumming, *Granite Crags* (Edinburgh and London, 1884), p. 143.

15 Frederick Jackson Turner, *The Frontier in American History* (New York, 1921), p. 1.

16 Bruce Bernstein, 'Foreword', in Bates and Lee, *Tradition and Innovation*, p. xvii.

17 George Wharton James, 'Basket Makers of California at Work', *The Basket: The Journal of the Basket Fraternity or Lovers of Indian Baskets and Other Good Things*, I/3 (July 1903), p. 6.

18 Beverly R. Ortiz and Julia F. Parker, *It Will Live Forever: Traditional Yosemite Indian Acorn Preparation* (Berkeley, CA, 1996; originally 1991), p. 3.

19 Bates and Lee, *Tradition and Innovation*, p. 163.

20 Alfred Runte, *Yosemite: The Embattled Wilderness* (Lincoln, NE, 1990), p. 144.

21 Alfred Runte, *National Parks: The American Experience* (Lanham, MD, 2010), p. 146.

22 Bates and Lee, *Tradition and Innovation*, pp. 104–5.

23 Boyd Cothran, 'Working the Indian Field Days: The Economy of Authenticity and the Question of Agency in Yosemite Valley', *American Indian Quarterly*, XXXIV/2 (Spring 2010), p. 194.

24 Brian Bibby, correspondence with the author, August 2011.

25 Jim Snyder, Yosemite National Park Historian (retired), correspondence with the author, February 2012.

26 See Bates and Lee, *Tradition and Innovation*; and Brian Bibby, *The Fine Art of California Indian Basketry*, exh. cat., Crocker Art Museum, Sacramento, California (Berkeley, CA, 1996).

27 Curtis, *The North American Indian*, vol. XIV, p. 133.

28 Quoted in Bates and Lee, *Tradition and Innovation*, p. 2.

29 Quoted ibid., p. 4.

30 Ibid., p. 115.

31 Bibby, 'Native American Art of the Yosemite Region', p. 103.

32 Bates and Lee, *Tradition and Innovation*, p. 114.

33 John Torigoe, 'Yosemite Basket Maker a Living Legend', www.cnn.com, 7 October 2009.

4 AMERICAN EDEN

1 Clarence King, *Mountaineering in the Sierra Nevada* (Boston, MA, 1872), p. 137.
2 M.I.W., 'The Yosemite', June 1866, typed copy, pp. 10–11, 15, Yosemite Research Library, Yosemite, California.
3 Francis P. Farquhar, ed., *The Ralston-Fry Wedding and the Wedding Journey to Yosemite, May 20, 1858, from the Diary of Miss Sarah Haight* (Berkeley, CA, 1961), p. 9.
4 James Mason Hutchings, 'The Yo-Ham-i-te Valley', *Hutchings' California Magazine*, I/1 (July 1856), p. 2.
5 Constance Gordon-Cumming, *Granite Crags* (Edinburgh and London, 1884), p. 257.
6 Ibid., p. 246.
7 Bayard Taylor, 'A Trip to the Big Trees', *North Pacific Review*, I/1 (October 1862), p. 19.
8 Willard B. Farwell, *Oration Delivered before the Society of California Pioneers, at their Celebration of the Eighth Anniversary of the Admission of the State of California into the Union* (Sacramento, CA, 1859), p. 12.
9 Walt Whitman, 'Song of the Redwood-tree', *Leaves of Grass* (Philadelphia, PA, 1882), p. 169.
10 See Sandra Sizer Frankiel, *California's Spiritual Frontiers: Religious Alternatives in Anglo-Protestantism, 1850–1910* (Berkeley, CA, 1988).
11 John Muir, *My First Summer in the Sierras* (Boston, MA, and New York, 1911), p. 336.
12 James Mason Hutchings, 'Diary', typed transcript, p. 91, Yosemite Research Library.
13 Lafayette Houghton Bunnell, *Discovery of the Yosemite, and the Indian War of 1851, Which Led to That Event* (Chicago, IL, 1880), p. 61.
14 Farquhar, ed., *The Ralston-Fry Wedding*, pp. 22–3.
15 James Mason Hutchings, *In the Heart of the Sierras* (Oakland, CA, 1886), p. 479.
16 Quoted in Kevin Starr, *Americans and the California Dream, 1850–1915* (New York, 1973), p. 101.
17 John Todd, *The Sunset Land; or, The Great Pacific Slope* (Boston, MA, 1871), pp. 119–20.
18 Mark Twain, *Roughing It* (Hartford, CT, 1873), pp. 170, 443.

19 Herbert L. Aulls, 'Over Foot Trails and Bridle Paths to Yo-Semite', 1876, manuscript, Denver Public Library, Colorado, pp. 1, 34.

20 See Edwin P. Whipple, ed., *Christianity and Humanity: A Series of Sermons by Thomas Starr King* (Boston, MA, 1878).

21 Quoted in David Wyatt, *The Fall into Eden: Landscape and Imagination in California* (New York, 1986), p. 33.

22 Muir, *My First Summer in the Sierras*, pp. 20–21.

23 Frankiel, *California's Spiritual Frontiers*, p. 120.

24 Quoted in Hans Huth, *Nature and the American: Three Centuries of Changing Attitudes*, 2nd edn (Lincoln, NE, 1990), p. 151.

25 James Bradley Thayer, *A Western Journey with Mr Emerson* (Boston, MA, 1884), p. 76.

26 Ralph Waldo Emerson to John Muir, 5 February 1872, from Concord, Massachusetts, typed copy, 1 page, Yosemite Research Library.

27 Theodore Roosevelt, *Outdoor Pastimes of an American Hunter* (New York, 1908), p. 316.

28 Clarence King, letter to Jim [Gardner] from New York, Spring [1860?], no. 27814, typed copy, p. 1; and King, letter to Jim from Yale, 19 September 1861, no. 27821, typed copy, p. 4, Huntington Library, San Marino, California.

29 Quoted in Starr, *Americans and the California Dream*, p. 427.

30 Herbert Hovencamp, *Science and Religion in America, 1800–1860* (Philadelphia, PA, 1978), p. x.

31 Quoted in Nancy K. Anderson and Linda S. Ferber, *Albert Bierstadt, Art and Enterprise,* exh. cat., Brooklyn Museum (New York, 1990), p. 178.

32 Fitz Hugh Ludlow, 'Letters from Sundown, No. v. The Artists' Western Expedition. Wanderings Here and There', New York *Evening Post* (24 October 1863), p. 1.

33 Quoted in John W. McCoubrey, *Sources and Documents in the History of Art Series* (Englewood Cliffs, NJ, 1965), pp. 111–12.

34 Ralph Waldo Emerson, 'Nature' [1836], in *American Literature Survey: The American Romantics, 1800–1860*, ed. Milton R. Stern and Seymour L. Gross (New York, 1968), pp. 240, 245.

35 Hutchings, *In the Heart of the Sierras*, pp. 355–6.

36 Hank Johnston, *The Yosemite Grant, 1864–1906: A Pictorial History* (Yosemite, CA, 1995), p. 248.

5 ARTISTS' MECCA

1 See Weston Naef et. al., *Era of Exploration: The Rise of Landscape Photography in the American West, 1860–1885*, exh. cat., Metropolitan Museum of Art, New York, and Albright-Knox Art Gallery, Buffalo (Boston, MA, 1975).

2 'Views in the Yosemite Valley', *Philadelphia Photographer*, III/28 (April 1866), p. 106.

3 Gordon Hendricks, *Eadweard Muybridge: The Father of the Motion Picture* (New York, 1975), p. 10.

4 Susan Coolidge, 'A Few Hints on the California Journey', *Scribner's Monthly*, VI/1 (May 1873), p. 29.

5 Helen Hunt Jackson, *Bits of Travel at Home* (Boston, MA, 1878), p. 86.

6 Fitz Hugh Ludlow, *The Heart of the Continent: A Record of Travel Across the Plains and in Oregon, with an Examination of the Mormon Principle* (New York, 1870), p. 419.

7 Ibid., p. 434.

8 Benjamin Parke Avery, 'Art Beginnings on the Pacific. I', *Overland Monthly*, I/1 (July 1868), p. 33; and Avery, 'Art Beginnings on the Pacific. II', I/2 (August 1868), p. 114.

9 Amelia Ransome Neville, *The Fantastic City: Memoirs of the Social and Romantic Life of Old San Francisco* (Boston, MA, and New York, 1932), p. 96.

10 'Photograph Studies: Eight Hundred Views of Yosemite Valley and the Big Trees', *Daily Alta California*, XXV/8410 (7 April 1873), p. 1.

11 'Art Notes', San Francisco *Morning Call* (18 January 1880); and John Wilmerding, *William Bradford, Artist of the Arctic: An Exhibition of his Paintings and Photographs*, exh. cat., deCordova and Dana Museum, Lincoln, and the Whaling Museum of New Bedford, Massachusetts (1969), p. 26.

12 [Exhibition review], *Boston Evening Transcript* (25 May 1872), p. 2. Courtesy Merl Moore, Research Collaborator, Smithsonian American Art Museum.

13 Constance Gordon-Cumming, *Granite Crags* (Edinburgh and London, 1884), pp. 282–3.

14 Louis H. Smaus, 'The Artists and Photographers of Yosemite (1855–1935), A Chronology', *Yosemite: Newsletter of the Yosemite Association*, XLIX/1 (Winter 1987), pp. 4–5; and Smaus, 'Yosemite in Stereo', *Yosemite*, LI/3 (Summer 1989), pp. 7–9.

15 Paul Hickman and Terence Pitts, *George Fiske: Yosemite Photographer* (Flagstaff, AZ, 1980), p. 24.

16 Peter E. Palmquist, *Shadowcatchers: A Directory of Women in California Photography*, vol. 1 (Arcata, CA, 1990), p. 70.

17 See ibid.; and 'Minutes of Commissioners' Meeting', 7 June 1888, *Committee on Tenements and Improvements of the Commission to Manage the Yosemite Grant and Mariposa Grove of Big Trees*, p. 165, California State Archive, Sacramento.

18 Craig D. Bates and Martha J. Lee, *Tradition and Innovation: A Basket History of the Indians of the Yosemite–Mono Lake Area* (Yosemite, CA, 1904), pp. 3–4.

19 Elizabeth H. Godfrey, 'Thumbnail Sketches of Yosemite Artists: Charles Dorman Robinson', *Yosemite Nature Notes*, XXIII/4 (April 1944), p. 39.

20 Katherine Mather Littell, *Chris Jorgensen: California Pioneer Artist* (Sonora, CA, 1988), p. 21.

21 Palmquist, *Shadowcatchers*, pp. 57–8.

22 See David Robertson, *West of Eden: A History of Art and Literature of Yosemite* (Yosemite, CA, 1984); and Ted Orland, *Man and Yosemite: A Photographer's View of the Early Years* (Santa Cruz, CA, 1985).

23 W. B. Lewis, Park Supervisor, letter to Mr J. T. Boysen, Yosemite, California, 20 May 1916, Yosemite Research Library, Yosemite, California.

24 Arthur C. Pillsbury, 'From One Air-craft to Another', *Sunset* (March 1910), pp. 343–6.

25 Jonathan Spaulding, *Ansel Adams and the American Landscape: A Biography* (Berkeley and Los Angeles, CA, and London, 1998), pp. 21–2.

26 'Bill Zorach Walking Under Big Tree, Yosemite', photograph number LC-USZ62-137265, Library of Congress; and two drawings by Zorach of himself with Ansel Adams (both numbered LC-USZ62-137883), Library of Congress.

27 Quoted in Robertson, *West of Eden*, p. 140.

28 Janice T. Driesbach and Susan Landauer, *Obata's Yosemite: The Art and Letters of Chiura Obata from His Trip to the High Sierra in 1927* (Yosemite, CA, 1993), p. 129.

29 Quoted in Roxana Robinson, *Georgia O'Keeffe: A Life* (New York, 1989), p. 425.

30 Robert Hughes, 'Master of the Yosemite', *Time*, CXIV/10, www.time.com, 3 September 1979.

31 'Ansel Adams Photograph Sells for Record $722,000', *The Telegraph*, www.telegraph.co.uk, 22 June 2010.

32 'History: Ansel Adams', www.sierraclub.org, accessed 4 April 2014.

33 'Charles Cramer – Biography', www.charlescramer.com, accessed 8 April 2014.

6 THE PARK IDEA

1 Hans Huth, 'Yosemite: The Story of an Idea', *Sierra Club Bulletin*, XXXIII/3 (March 1948).

2 Hans Huth, *Nature and the American: Three Centuries of Changing Attitudes*, 2nd edn (Lincoln, NE, 1990), pp. 66ff.

3 Alan Tate, *Great City Parks* (London, 2001), pp. 73ff.

4 Horace Greeley, 'An Overland Journey. XXIX. California – The Yosemite. Bear Valley, Cal., Aug. 14, 1859', New York *Tribune* (23 September 1859); from transcript, p. 10, Yosemite Research Library, Yosemite, California.

5 Joseph Hutchinson, San Francisco, letter to his father, 7 June 1859; quoted from transcript, p. 10, Yosemite Research Library.

6 Brantz Mayer, letter to Cornelia Poor Mayer, 28 June 1872, p. 1, HM 21313; and Mayer, undated letter, pp. 2–3, HM 21211, Huntington Library, San Marino, California.

7 Hank Johnston, *The Yosemite Grant, 1864–1906: A Pictorial History* (Yosemite, CA, 1995), pp. 52–5; and Huth, 'Yosemite: The Story of an Idea', pp. 66–8.

8 Laura Wood Roper, *FLO: A Biography of Frederick Law Olmsted* [1973] (Baltimore, MD, 1983), p. 268.

9 Margaret Sanborn, *Yosemite: Its Discovery, its Wonders, and its People* (New York, 1981), p. 99; and Johnston, *The Yosemite Grant*, p. 55.

10 John Todd, *The Sunset Land; or, The Great Pacific Slope* (Boston, MA, 1871), p. 115.

11 Clarence King, *Mountaineering in the Sierra Nevada* (Boston, MA, 1872), p. 138.

12 Peter E. Palmquist, *Carleton E. Watkins, Photographer of the American West*, exh. cat., Amon Carter Museum, Fort Worth, Texas (Albuquerque, NM, 1983), p. 19.

13 Nancy K. Anderson, *Cho-looke, The Yosemite Fall*, exh. cat., Timken Art Gallery, San Diego (1986), n.p.

14 *National Park Service Cultural Landscapes Inventory: Mariposa Grove, Yosemite National Park* (2004), Part 2a, p. 4, www.nps.gov, accessed 26 July 2012.

15 Quoted in Alfred Runte, *Yosemite: The Embattled Wilderness* (Lincoln, NE, 1990), p. 28.

16 Huth, 'Yosemite: The Story of an Idea', pp. 70–71.

17 Laura Wood Roper, 'The Yosemite Valley and the Mariposa Big Trees: A Preliminary Report (1865) by Frederick Law Olmsted', *Landscape Architecture*, XLIII/1 (October 1952), pp. 12–25.

18 Shirley Sargent, *Galen Clark: Yosemite Guardian* (San Francisco, CA, 1964).

19 John Muir, 'The Bee-pastures of California', *The Century Magazine*, XXIV (July 1882), p. 228.

20 John Muir, 'The Treasures of the Yosemite', *The Century Magazine*, XL/4 (August 1890), pp. 483–500; and John Muir, 'Features of the Proposed Yosemite National Park', *The Century Magazine*, XL/5 (September 1890), pp. 656–67.

21 George G. Mackenzie, Lucius P. Deming and Robert Underwood Johnson, 'Destructive Tendencies in the Yosemite Valley', *The Century Magazine*, XXXIX/3 (January 1890), pp. 476, 478.

22 'Amateur Management of the Yosemite Scenery', *The Century Magazine*, XL/5 (September 1890), p. 798.

23 Quoted in Alfred Runte, 'Promoting the Golden West: Advertising and the Railroad', *California History*, LXX/1 (Spring 1991), p. 63.

24 Harvey Meyerson, 'Forgotten Legacy: U.S. Army Environmentalists at Yosemite', *Journal of the West*, XXXVIII/1 (January 1999), pp. 40ff.

25 Meyerson, 'Forgotten Legacy', p. 43.

26 Theodore Roosevelt, *Outdoor Pastimes of an American Hunter* [1905] (New York, 1908), p. 315.

27 Douglas Brinkley, *The Wilderness Warrior: Theodore Roosevelt and the Crusade for America* (New York, 2009), p. 540.

28 Runte, *Yosemite*, p. 85.

29 'The John Muir Exhibit', www.sierraclub.org, accessed 10 March 2014.

30 'National Park Entrance Fees to be Waived over Veterans Day Weekend to Inspire National Unity, Hope and Healing', www.home.nps.gov, 4 October 2001.

7 TOURISTS, TOLLS AND TRAINS

1 John Muir, 'The Summer Flood of Tourists,' San Francisco *Daily Evening Bulletin* (14 June 1875).

2 Clarence King, *Mountaineering in the Sierra Nevada* (Boston, MA, 1872), p. 149.

3 Quoted in Oscar T. Shuck, comp., *The California Scrap-book: A Repository of Useful Information and Select Reading* (San Francisco, CA, 1869), p. 550.

4 Emilie Sussman, *My Trip to Yosemite: From the Journal of Emilie Sussman, 1872* (San Francisco, CA, 1939), p. 7.

5 *Nelson's Pictorial Guide-books: The Yosemite Valley, and the Mammoth Trees and Geysers of California* (New York, 1870), p. 16.

6 Brantz Mayer, letter to his wife Cornelia (Poor) Mayer, 28 June 1872, from Yosemite, manuscript, pp. 6, 12, Huntington Library, San Marino, California.

7 Dio Lewis, *Gypsies; or, Why We went Gypsying in the Sierras* (Boston, MA, 1881), p. 156.

8 Hank Johnston, *The Yosemite Grant, 1864–1906: A Pictorial History* (Yosemite, CA, 1995), pp. 32–3.

9 Alfred Runte, *Yosemite: The Embattled Wilderness* (Lincoln, NE, 1990), p. 17.

10 Mrs E. S. Carr, entry for 1873, *Grand Register of the Cosmopolitan Bathhouse and Saloon*, Yosemite Research Library, Yosemite, California.

11 Johnston, *The Yosemite Grant*, p. 162.

12 Mayer, 'Yosemite Notes', 1872, manuscript, HM4279, pp. 1–2, Huntington Library.

13 Constance Gordon-Cumming, *Granite Crags* (Edinburgh and London, 1884), p. 261.

14 Susanna B. Dakin, *Yo Semite 1878 Adventures of N & C: Journal and Drawings by Carrie E. LeConte* (San Francisco, CA, 1944), p. 27.

15 James Mason Hutchings, 'The Great Yo Semite Valley', *Hutchings' California Magazine*, IV/4 (October 1859), p. 154.

16 Anne Maria Bythewood Trescot, letter to her daughter, Eliza Josephine Trescot Simkins, 26 [May?] [1876?], pp. 3–4, Huntington Library.

17 Linda Wedel Greene, *Yosemite: The Park and its Resources* (Yosemite, CA, 1987), pp. 92ff.

18 Mary E. Blake, *On the Wing: Rambling Notes of a Trip to the Pacific* (Boston, MA, 1883), p. 129.

19 James Mason Hutchings, *In the Heart of the Sierras: The Yo Semite Valley, both Historical and Descriptive; and Scenes by the Way* (Oakland, CA, 1886), p. 350; and Caroline M. Churchill, *Over the Purple Hills; or, Sketches of Travel in California* (Denver, CO, 1883), pp. 142–3.

20 Nancy Anderson, 'The Kiss of Enterprise: The Western Landscape as Symbol and Resource', in *The West as America: Reinterpreting Images of the Frontier, 1820–1920*, ed. William H. Truettner, exh. cat., National Museum of American Art, Washington, DC (1991), p. 277.

21 Joshua Scott Johns, 'The Parks in Railroad Advertising: Empire Building, 1873–1885', American Studies, University of Virginia, http://xroads.virginia.edu/~ma96/railroad, accessed 17 June 2011.

22 Ibid.

23 Joshua Scott Johns, 'The Parks in Railroad Advertising: Expanding the Target Market, 1885–1900', *American Studies*, Universtiy of Virginia, http://xroads.virginia.edu/~ma96/railroad, accessed 14 April 2015.

24 Greene, *Yosemite: The Park and its Resources*, pp. 713–14.

25 Quoted in Frank A. Sternad, 'Where Only the Fearless Dare to Stand: Yosemite's Overhanging Rock', *San Francisco Bay Area Post Card Club Newsletter*, XIX/2 (February 2004), p. 8, www.postcard.org.

26 Ann G. Harris, Esther Tuttle and Sherwood D. Tuttle, *Geology of National Parks*, 6th edn (Dubuque, IA, 2004), p. 388; and 'National Park Notes: National Parks and Reservations', *Sierra Club Bulletin*, X/1 (January 1916), p. 105.

27 Kevin Starr, *Sunset Magazine: A Century of Western Living, 1898–1998* (Stanford, CA, 1998), pp. 58, 210–11.

28 Tom Bopp, 'Vintage Songs of Yosemite', www.yosemitemusic.com, accessed 15 August 2011.

29 'Studebaker Car Driven to Very Edge of Famous Overhanging Rock: Automobile Figures in Unequaled Feat in History of the Yosemite', *San Francisco Examiner* (17 September 1916), p. 31.

30 Quoted in William Robert Lowry, *Repairing Paradise: The Restoration of Nature in America's National Parks* (Washington, DC, 2009), p. 67.

31 John Steele Gordon, *An Empire of Wealth: The Epic History of American Economic Power* (New York, 2004), pp. 298–9.

32 Amy Scott, 'Revisiting Yosemite', *Yosemite: Art of an American Icon*, exh. cat., Autry National Center (Los Angeles, CA, 2006), p. 163.

33 'Badger Pass Ski Resort', www.trails.com, accessed 15 March 2014.

34 Gordon T. McClelland and Jay T. Last, *California Orange Box Labels* (Beverly Hills, CA, 1985), pp. 37, 90–91.

35 Merrill Ann Wilson, 'Rustic Architecture: The National Park Style', *Trends* (July–August–September 1976), p. 4.

36 Scott, 'Revisiting Yosemite', p. 163.

37 'Yosemite National Park: Ahwahnee Hotel', www.yosemitehikes.com, accessed 27 August 2012.

38 'The Bracebridge Dinner at Yosemite', www.bracebridgedinners.com, accessed 15 January 2014.

39 John Muir to Jeanne Carr, 29 May 1870, quoted in John Muir, *Letters to a Friend: Written to Mrs Ezra S. Carr, 1866–1879* (Boston, MA, and New York, 1915), p. 81.

8 TROUBLE IN PARADISE

1 Richard W. Righter, *The Battle over Hetch Hetchy: America's Most Controversial Dam and the Birth of Environmentalism* (New York, 2005).

2 John Muir, *The Yosemite* (New York, 1912), pp. 249–50.

3 See Warren Olney, 'Water Supply for the Cities about the Bay of San Francisco', and E. T. Parsons, 'Proposed Destruction of Hetch-Hetchy', *Out West*, XXXI/1 (July 1909), pp. 599–626.

4 Muir, *The Yosemite*, p. 262.

5 Char Miller, *Gifford Pinchot and the Making of Modern Environmentalism* (Washington, DC, 2001), p. 5.

6 Quoted in Roderick Nash, *Wilderness and the American Mind*, 4th edn (New Haven, CT, 2001), p. 161.

7 Nash, *Wilderness and the American Mind*, p. 182.

8 William Cronon, *Uncommon Ground: Rethinking the Human Place in Nature* (New York, 1995), p. 25.

9 Alfred Runte, *Yosemite: The Embattled Wilderness* (Lincoln, NE, 1990), pp. 144ff.

10 Linda Wedel Greene, *Yosemite: The Park and its Resources* (Yosemite, CA, 1987), pp. 448–9.

11 Ibid., p. 525.

12 Runte, *Yosemite,* p. 183.

13 NPS Historic Photograph Collection', www.nps.gov, accessed 3 April 2014. Catalogue numbers HPC-000207 and HPC-000074.

14 Greene, *Yosemite: The Park and its Resources*, pp. 752–3.

15 Danny Palmerlee and Beth Kohn, *Yosemite, Sequoia and Kings Canyon National Parks* (Oakland, CA, 2008), p. 118.

16 Bob R. O'Brien, *Our National Parks and the Search for Sustainability* (Austin, TX, 1999), p. 178.

17 Quoted ibid.

18 'U.S. Picks Concessionaire for Yosemite Park', *New York Times*, www.nytimes.com, 18 December 1992.

19 Ibid.

20 Brian Melley, 'Yosemite: Tough Task Ahead for New Superintendent', www.seattlepi.com, 5 February 2003.

21 Bettina Boxall, 'Yosemite Plan Calls for More Campsites and Parking Spaces', *Los Angeles Times*, http://articles.latimes.com, 9 January 2013.

22 Scott Gediman, Media Relations Office, Yosemite National Park, correspondence with the author, 2011.

23 Information courtesy of Scott Gediman.

24 'Yosemite National Park: Invasive Plants', www.nps.gov, accessed
10 January 2014.

25 'Summary of 2011 Work', *Invasive Plant Management Program 2012
Work Plan* (Yosemite, CA, 2011), p. 5, www.nps.gov, accessed 18 February
2012.

26 'Yosemite National Park: Vegetation Map', www.nps.gov, accessed
1 August 2011.

27 'Yosemite National Park: Air Quality', www.nps.gov, accessed 22 August
2011.

28 Palmerlee and Kohn, *Yosemite, Sequoia and Kings Canyon National Parks*,
p. 84.

29 Thomas A. Smith, *I'm Just a Seasonal: The Life of a Seasonal Ranger in
Yosemite National Park* (Rochester, NY, 2005), p. 37.

30 Jesse McKinley and Ian Lovett, 'At Yosemite, 18 Reminders of Dangers
of the Outdoors', *New York Times*, www.nytimes.com, 5 September 2011.

31 Jane Engle, 'Yosemite Half Dome's New Lottery Permit System Begins',
Los Angeles Times, http://articles.latimes.com, 4 March 2012.

9 A NATIONAL PLAYGROUND

1 Laura Wood Roper, 'The Yosemite Valley and the Mariposa Big Trees:
A Preliminary Report (1865) by Frederick Law Olmsted', *Landscape
Architecture*, XLIII/1 (October 1952), p. 22.

2 'Yosemite National Park: Park Statistics', www.nps.gov, accessed 1 August
2013.

3 Jack McCallum, 'Who Needs an Airplane', *Sports Illustrated* (26 August
1985), www.sportsillustrated.cnn.com, accessed 1 August 2011.

4 Lauren Smiley, 'BASE Jumper Won't Stop Illegal Leaps Despite Yosemite
Tasing', *SF Weekly News* (9 February 2011), www.sfweekly.com, accessed
19 September 2013.

5 'An Unparalleled Feat', San Francisco *Bulletin* (19 October 1875), p. 3.

6 Jim Herson, 'Half Dome Redux, 7/5/11', www.vocr.sri.com, 5 July 2011.

7 'Yosemite National Park: Half Dome Permits for Day Hiking',
www.nps.gov, accessed 10 January 2012.

8 Rick Deutsch, *Yosemite's Half Dome: Everything you Need to Know to
Successfully Hike Yosemite's Most Famous Landmark* (Berkeley, CA, 2007).

9 Rick Deutsch, correspondence with the author, 29 November 2012;
9 April 2014.

10 Bob Madgic, *Shattered Air: A True Account of Catastrophe and Courage
on Yosemite's Half Dome* (Short Hills, NJ, 2005).

11 'From a Lady Correspondent. Yosemite Valley, June 1858' (16 June 1858), typescript, p. 2, Yosemite Research Library, Yosemite, California.

12 Francis P. Farquhar, ed., *The Ralston-Fry Wedding and the Wedding Journey to Yosemite, May 20, 1858, from the Diary of Miss Sarah Haight* (Berkeley, CA, 1961).

13 Virginia Best Adams, 'Best's Studio', in *Yosemite: Saga of a Century, 1864–1964*, ed. Jack Gyer (Oakhurst, CA, 1964), pp. 46–7.

14 Mary Street Alinder, *Ansel Adams: A Biography* (New York, 1998), p. 56.

15 'The Ansel Adams Gallery: Photography Workshops', www.anseladams.com, accessed 16 March 2011.

16 'Yosemite Renaissance XXVIII Prospectus', www.yosemiterenaissance.org, accessed 9 April 2014.

17 'David Hockney (b. 1937), Merced River, Yosemite Valley, September 1982', Christie's New York, Sale 2522/Lot 244, www.christies.com, 7 April 2011.

18 Claire Cain Miller, 'iPad is an Artist's Canvas for David Hockney', *New York Times*, http://bits.blogs.nytimes.com, 10 January 2014.

19 Tony Foster, 'Sacred Places: Watercolour Diaries from the American Southwest', *Gerald Peters Gallery Newsletter* (Santa Fe, NM, Spring 2011), p. 1.

20 'The Collaborative Works of Mark Klett and Byron Wolfe', www.klettandwolfe.com, accessed 14 January 2011.

21 Jennifer A. Watts, 'Photography's Workshop: Yosemite in the Modern Era', in *Yosemite: Art of an American Icon*, ed. Amy Scott, exh. cat., Autry National Center (Los Angeles, CA, 2006), pp. 115–16.

22 'Yosemite National Park: Fees and Regulations', www.nps.gov, accessed 10 January 2014. See 'Did You Know?' at bottom of page.

23 Jane Alexiadis, 'What's it Worth? Ansel Adams' Tin Can Print', *San Jose Mercury News*, www.mercurynews.com, 24 June 2011.

24 Eric Peter Nash, *Ansel Adams: The Spirit of Wild Places* (New York, 2009), p. 62.

25 Ibid.

Select Bibliography

Anderson, Nancy K., and Linda S. Ferber, *Albert Bierstadt: Art and Enterprise*, exh. cat., Brooklyn Museum (New York, 1990)

Bates, Craig D., and Martha J. Lee, *Tradition and Innovation: A Basket History of the Indians of the Yosemite–Mono Lake Area* (Yosemite, CA, 1990)

Bibby, Brian, *The Fine Art of California Indian Basketry*, exh. cat., Crocker Art Museum, Sacramento, CA (Berkeley, CA, 1996)

Bunnell, Lafayette Houghton, *Discovery of the Yosemite, and the Indian War of 1851, Which Led to That Event* (Chicago, IL, 1880)

Clark, Galen, *Indians of the Yosemite Valley and Vicinity* (Yosemite, CA, 1904)

Cronon, William, *Uncommon Ground: Rethinking the Human Place in Nature* (New York, 1995)

Deutsch, Rick, *Yosemite's Half Dome: Everything You Need to Know to Successfully Hike Yosemite's Most Famous Landmark* (Berkeley, CA, 2007)

Glazner, Allen F., and Greg M. Stock, *Geology Underfoot in Yosemite National Park* (Missoula, MT, 2010)

Gordon-Cumming, Constance, *Granite Crags* (Edinburgh and London, 1884)

Greene, Linda Wedel, *Yosemite: The Park and its Resources* (Yosemite, CA, 1987)

Huber, N. King, *The Geologic Story of Yosemite National Park* (Washington, DC, 1987)

Hutchings, James Mason, *Scenes of Wonder and Curiosity in California* (San Francisco, CA, 1862)

—, *In the Heart of the Sierras: The Yo Semite Valley, Both Historical and Descriptive; and Scenes by the Way* (Oakland, CA, 1886)

Huth, Hans, *Nature and the American: Three Centuries of Changing Attitudes*, 2nd edn (Lincoln, NE, 1990)

Johnston, Hank, *The Yosemite Grant, 1864–1906: A Pictorial History* (Yosemite, CA, 1995)

King, Clarence, *Mountaineering in the Sierra Nevada* (Boston, MA, 1872)

La Pena, Frank, Craig D. Bates and Stephen P. Medley, comps, *Legends of the Yosemite Miwok* [1981] (Yosemite, CA, 1993)

Lowry, William Robert, *Repairing Paradise: The Restoration of Nature in America's National Parks* (Washington, DC, 2009)

Ludlow, Fitz Hugh, *The Heart of the Continent: A Record of Travel across the Plains and in Oregon, with an Examination of the Mormon Principle* (New York, 1870)

Muir, John, *My First Summer in the Sierra* (Boston, MA, and New York, 1911)

—, *The Yosemite* (New York, 1912)

Naef, Weston, et. al., *Era of Exploration: The Rise of Landscape Photography in the American West, 1860–1885*, exh. cat., Metropolitan Museum of Art, New York, and Albright-Knox Art Gallery, Buffalo, NY (Boston, MA, 1975)

Nash, Roderick, *Wilderness and the American Mind*, 4th edn (New Haven, CT, 2001)

O'Brien, Bob R., *Our National Parks and the Search for Sustainability* (Austin, TX, 1999)

Orland, Ted, *Man and Yosemite: A Photographer's View of the Early Years* (Santa Cruz, CA, 1985).

Ortiz, Beverly R., and Julia F. Parker, *It Will Live Forever: Traditional Yosemite Indian Acorn Preparation* [1991] (Berkeley, CA, 1996)

Palmerlee, Danny, and Beth Kohn, *Yosemite, Sequoia and Kings Canyon National Parks* (Oakland, CA, 2008)

Powers, Stephen, *Tribes of California* (Washington, DC, 1877)

Robertson, David, *West of Eden: A History of Art and Literature of Yosemite* (Yosemite, CA, 1984)

Runte, Alfred, *National Parks: The American Experience* (Lanham, MD, 2010)

—, *Yosemite: The Embattled Wilderness* (Lincoln, NE, 1990)

Sanborn, Margaret, *Yosemite: Its Discovery, its Wonders, and its People* (New York, 1981)

Sargent, Shirley, *Galen Clark: Yosemite Guardian* (San Francisco, CA, 1964)

Schaffer, Jeffrey P., *Yosemite National Park: A Natural History Guide to Yosemite and its Trails* (Berkeley, CA, 1983)

Scott, Amy, ed., *Yosemite: Art of an American Icon*, exh. cat., Autry National Center, Los Angeles (Los Angeles, CA, 2006)

Smith, Michael L., *Pacific Visions: California Scientists and the Environment, 1850–1915* (New Haven, CT, 1987)

Spence, Mark David, *Dispossessing the Wilderness: Indian Removal and the Making of the National Parks* (New York and Oxford, 1999)

Starr, Kevin, *Americans and the California Dream, 1850–1915*
    (New York, 1973)
Whitney, Josiah D., *Geology of California*, vol. 1: *Report of Progress and
    Synopsis of the Field-work, from 1860 to 1864* (Philadelphia, PA, 1865)
Wuerthner, George, *Yosemite: A Visitor's Companion* (Mechanicsburg, PA, 1994)

Acknowledgements

I am grateful to Michael Leaman, Publisher, and Daniel Allen for the opportunity to contribute *Yosemite* to Reaktion Books' impressive catalogue. Also at the top of my list is the late Peter Palmquist, who knew more about nineteenth-century California photographers than I ever will. Brian Bibby graciously answered questions and offered suggestions on a variety of topics related to Native American basketry and the culture surrounding it.

At the Yosemite Research Museum and Library, Barbara Beroza, Chief Curator, and Linda Eade, Librarian (now retired), have always been immensely helpful. James B. Snyder, former Park Historian, continued to answer my questions despite his retirement, and Scott Gediman in the Public Affairs Office very kindly answered a variety of questions. Greg Stock, Yosemite Park Geologist, graciously conferred on geological issues, as did Michael Hozik at Stockton University. Robert Woolard and Tom Bopp, experts on Yosemite art and music, respectively, were extremely helpful, as was Rick Deutsch, who answered questions about climbing Half Dome.

Several colleagues at Stockton University generously read and made suggestions on sections of the manuscript. They include Dick Colby, Deborah Gussman, Lisa Honaker, Michael Hozik, Elaine Ingulli, Lance Olsen, Lisa Rosner and Joseph Rubenstein. Dick Colby provided information on the Sierra Club and science topics, and Sandy Bierbrauer gave me tips on botanical nomenclature. Louise Tillstrom, Principal Library Assistant at Stockton and neighbour extraordinaire, delivered books to my doorstep.

I am very grateful to all of the institutions, photographers and collectors who allowed me to reproduce their images of Yosemite subjects. Dan Anderson, proprietor of the website Yosemite Online Library, allowed me to use scanned images, and Michael Schroeder helped me to identify the artist Gilbert Munger in old photographs. Amy Elizabeth Burton, in the Office of the u.s. Senate Curator, worked persistently to obtain permission for me to use a photograph of President Obama's inaugural luncheon. My sincerest thanks to all of you.